Practice Book

Practice Book

Written by Len Frobisher

Edited by Mike Askew and Sheila Ebbutt

Rigby
Halley Court, Jordan Hill, Oxford, OX2 8EJ
a division of Reed Educational and Professional Publishing Ltd

Rigby is a registered trademark of Reed Educational and Professional Publishing Ltd

OXFORD MELBOURNE AUCKLAND
JOHANNESBURG BLANTYRE GABORONE
IBADAN PORTSMOUTH (NH) CHICAGO

© Rigby 1999
Written by Len Frobisher
Edited by Mike Askew and Sheila Ebbutt

Rigby. All rights reserved. No part of this publication may be reproduced in any material form (including photocopying or storing it in any medium by electronic means and whether or not transiently or incidentally to some other use of this publication) without the prior written permission of the copyright owner, except in accordance with the provisions of the Copyright, Designs and Patents Act 1988 or under the terms of a licence issued by the Copyright Licensing Agency, 90 Tottenham Court Road, London W1P 0LP. Applications for the copyright owner's written permission to reproduce any part of this publication should be addressed in the first instance to the publisher.

First published 1999

04 03 02 01 00
10 9 8 7 6 5 4 3

ISBN 0 435 21676 7

Designed and typeset by Gecko Limited, Bicester, Oxon
Illustrated by Gecko Limited and Harvey Collins
Printed and bound by Scotprint, Scotland

Introduction

Children need two different kinds of practice to consolidate their mathematics learning:

- guided practice (teacher-led support to help with new ideas)
- independent practice (to consolidate knowledge and skills already learned).

To help distinguish between these types of practice, **Numeracy Focus** provides its practice resources in separate books. This *Practice Book* provides the opportunity for independent practice.

Once children have learned the mathematics, they need time for independent practice so they can consolidate their ideas and their skills become fluent. The *Practice Book* is designed for children to have short periods of focused practice with an emphasis on speed as well as accuracy.

The exercises in the *Practice Book* provide material for two sessions of practice a week, each lasting about 10 to 15 minutes. The content of each session is derived from material taught in the *Teaching and Learning File* during the previous 4–6 weeks. This allows time for children to consolidate their learning and to be ready to practise it with some fluency. To assist this, and promote confidence, the questions are set at a slightly easier level than the material actually taught.

The content of the *Practice Book* pages is mixed, drawing on the range of skills and knowledge children build on during the year. There is an emphasis on numerical skills, together with a smaller range of questions on measures, shape and space, and data handling. The first exercise for each session consists of quick calculation questions. The last question is generally more open-ended, offering children scope to apply their mathematics knowledge more flexibly.

Attached to some of the exercises is a hint box. Hint boxes contain tips and examples to help children work out answers.

The material is presented in a range of formats, which will have been introduced to children during the lessons and in the accompanying activities in the *Teaching and Learning File*. It is important that children become used to different ways of presenting mathematics exercises and problems so that they learn the skills of extracting information and making sense of written tasks. Children will have learned specific mathematical vocabulary during mathematics lessons and they should understand and know how to use it.

Children record their answers to *Practice Book* questions in an exercise book. In order to set out their work clearly and to help with the drawing of tables and charts, this book should be the standard mathematics exercise book bound with squared paper. As the *Practice Book* is designed for children to practise aspects of mathematics they are more confident with, they can be encouraged to pay more attention to the setting out of their work. This exercise book can offer a more 'public' presentation of their mathematics, and children should be encouraged to work clearly, neatly and systematically.

Numeracy Focus 4: Practice Book

Practice 1a

1 Copy these and complete them.

1. 8 + 3 = ___
2. 19 − 6 = ___
3. 17 + 17 = ___
4. 90 − 30 = ___
5. 16 add 20
6. 90 plus 10
7. 17 take away 9
8. 51 minus 49
9. Add 20, 50 and 10

2 Add pairs of numbers that are next to each other in the grid. Make all 12 possible additions.

3	4	5
1	2	3
5	2	6

1 + 5 = 6
3 + 1 = 4

3 Copy these and complete them.

1. 7 + 3 − 3 = ___
2. 14 + 5 − ___ = 14
3. 29 + ___ − 6 = 29
4. ___ + 17 − 17 = 8
5. 16 + 28 − ___ = 16
6. 63 + ___ − 49 = 63

4 Copy these addition walls and write the missing numbers.

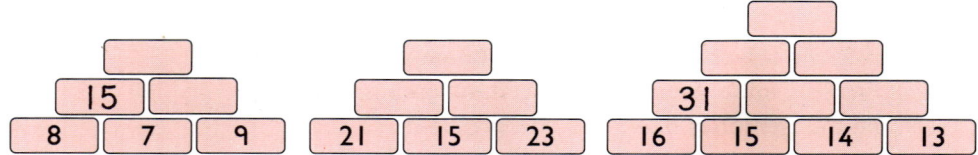

5 Copy the diagram six times. Use these numbers in the start circle.

| 6 | 16 | 34 | 40 | 81 | 98 |

Complete the diagrams. What do you notice? Write about it. Explain why it happens.

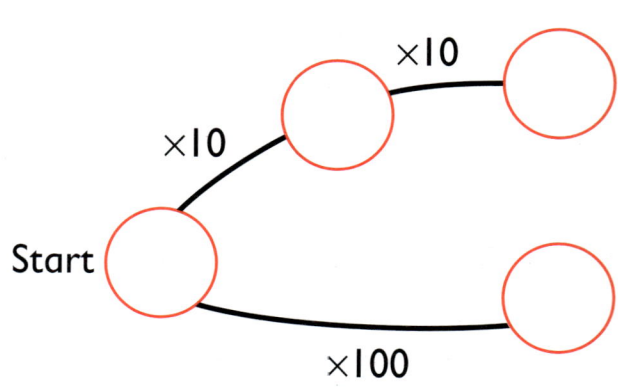

Practice 1b

1 Copy these and write the missing numbers.

1. $12 + 8 = \square$
2. $\square + 3 = 13$
3. $17 - 9 = \square$
4. $\square - 13 = 7$
5. $6 + 8 + 2 = \square$
6. $5 + \square + 8 = 18$
7. $\square \times 9 = 18$
8. $5 \times \square = 35$
9. $24 \div 4 = \square$

2 Copy these subtraction grids and fill in the missing numbers.

−	5	9
4		
2		

−	8	6
3		
5		

−	7	4
4		
2		

−	9	8
7		
5		

−	7	6
6		
1		

3 Copy this grid.

10 more	25									
number	15	49	500	190	1000	32	231	708	97
10 less	5									

In the top row write the number which is 10 more.
In the bottom row write the number which is 10 less.

4
1. Write three additions which each make 7.
2. Write four additions which each make 8.
3. Write four additions which each make 9.
4. Write five additions which each make 10.

5 Which numbers should be written in the empty triangles?

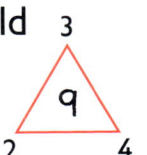
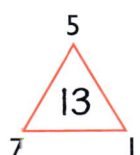
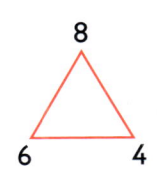
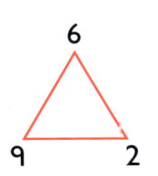
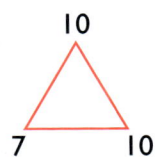

Numeracy Focus 4: Practice Book

Practice 2a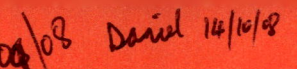

1 Copy these and complete them.

1. 4 + 7 = ___
2. 12 − 5 = ___
3. Add 30 to 40
4. 79 subtract 50
5. 4 times 6
6. Share 16 between 2
7. 473 + 6 = ___
8. 718 − 5 = ___
9. 2 × 3 = ___

2 Choose a number from each circle to make an addition.

Make four more additions.

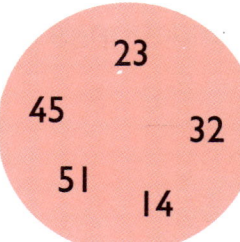 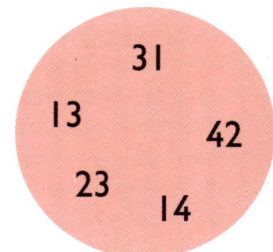

3 Copy these diagrams. Multiply the numbers which are next to each other.

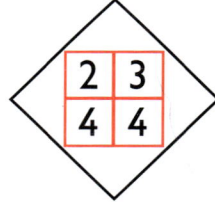 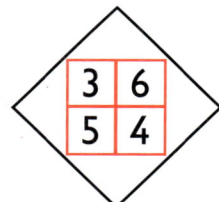 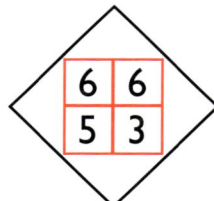 

4 Copy this shape. Draw the lengths accurately.

Measure the length marked with a ? on your drawing. Write it to the nearest centimetre.

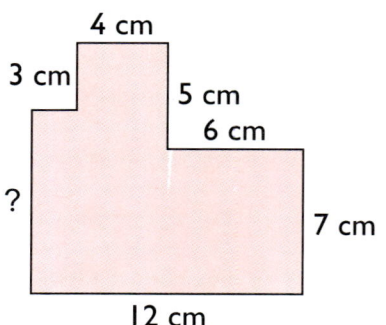

5 Choose two numbers from the rectangle to make a fraction less than 1.

Make four more fractions that are less than 1.

Practice 2b

1 Copy these and write the missing numbers.

1. 20 ÷ ☐ = 4
2. 3 + 9 + ☐ = 13
3. ☐ + 6 = 17
4. 3 × ☐ = 15
5. 12 ÷ ☐ = 4
6. 13 − 5 = ☐
7. 7 + ☐ = 12
8. ☐ − 18 = 2
9. ☐ ÷ 10 = 10

2 Copy the grid. Divide each number by 10 and write the answer in the row below.

20	100	420	50	900	30	170	550
2							

3 Copy the three sentences.

Use the seven numbers in the circle to make the sentences true.

☐ is less than ☐.

☐ is more than ☐.

☐ is between ☐ and ☐.

Do this three times.

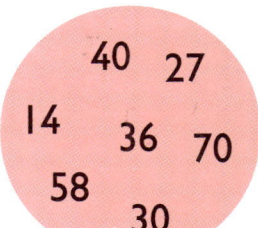

40 27 14 36 70 58 30

4 Write out the pairs of calculations which have the same answer.

2 × 3	9 × 1	5 × 4	7 × 2	4 × 3
36 ÷ 4	12 ÷ 2	28 ÷ 2	36 ÷ 3	100 ÷ 5

5 Carla has a £1 coin and two other coins in her purse.

List ten different amounts of money that she might have.

Numeracy Focus 4: Practice Book

Practice 3a 30/09/08

1 Copy these and complete them.

1. Double 18
2. 17 − 9 = ___
3. 166 + 9 = ___
4. 900 − 1 = ___
5. 148 − 11 = ___
6. Half of 900
7. 200 − 8 = ___
8. 400 + 37 = ___
9. 70 ÷ 10 = ___

2 Copy these subtraction grids and fill in the missing numbers.

−	37	59
16	21	
24		35

−	86	28
15		
23		

−	99	78
46		
57		

−	74	85
31		
62		

3 Copy the sentences. Choose numbers from the box to make the sentences true. Use each number only once.

☐ is less than ☐ .

☐ is more than ☐ .

☐ is between ☐ and ☐ .

17 28 49 29 62 50 70

4 Find the answers.   *Look for patterns.*

70 + 20
60 + 30
50 + 40

65 + 15
55 + 15
45 + 15

90 − 10
80 − 20
70 − 30

35 − 25
55 − 25
75 − 25

5 Use the numbers in the circle to make the additions. You may use the numbers more than once.

___ + ___ = 58   ___ + ___ = 77

___ + ___ = 69   ___ + ___ = 86

Circle: 62, 26, 34, 24, 43

Numeracy Focus 4: Practice Book

Practice 3b

1 Copy these and write the missing numbers.

1. 376 − ☐ = 371
2. 14 ÷ 2 = ☐
3. 4 × 6 = ☐
4. ☐ + 28 = 528
5. 83 + ☐ = 91
6. ☐ + 8 = 35
7. ☐ × 2 = 20
8. ☐ ÷ 5 = 10
9. ☐ − 7 = 393

2 Measure these lines. Write the lengths to the nearest centimetre.

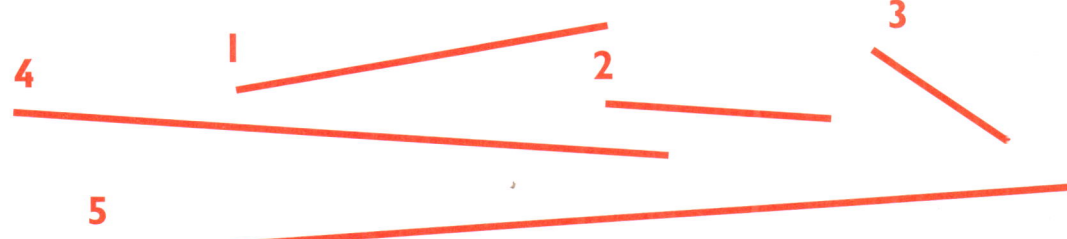

3 Choose a number from each circle.
Make an addition and write down the answer.
Do this six times.

Circle 1: 21, 32, 14
Circle 2: 42, 54, 33, 65

4 Choose two numbers from the box.
Make a multiplication and write down the answer.
Do this ten times.

2   3   4   5   6   10

5 Make up your own rule for this sequence.
Find the missing numbers.

2   5   ☐   ☐   ☐   ☐

Make up a rule for another sequence with the same two starting numbers.

Numeracy Focus 4: Practice Book

Practice 4a

1 Copy these and complete them.

1. 50 + 80 = ____
2. 700 + 300 = ____
3. 3 multiplied by 7
4. From 27 take 7
5. The sum of 37 and 15
6. 70 + 52 = ____
7. One quarter of 32
8. 700 ÷ 10 = ____
9. Twice 400

2 Choose a number from each circle to make a division. Write it down. Make five more.

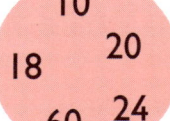

Circle 1: 10, 18, 20, 60, 24
Circle 2: 2, 4, 6, 5, 10, 3
Circle 3: 4, 5, 6

3 Copy these and complete them.

17 —double→ ☐ —double→ ☐   17 —×4→ ☐
30 —double→ ☐ —double→ ☐   30 —×4→ ☐
25 —double→ ☐ —double→ ☐   25 —×4→ ☐

4 Choose a number from row 1 and add it to a number from row 2 to make an answer in row 3. Make five more.

24 + 17 = 41

row 1	(24)	47	65	74	16	28	43	52	37	29
row 2	26	29	25	(17)	38	18	49	17	18	44
row 3	65	92	(41)	73	61	54	73	53	91	90

5 Use each of these digits once only to make four 3-digit numbers. Put the four numbers in order.

1 5 3 6 7
9 4 2 1 2 3 8

Numeracy Focus 4: Practice Book

Practice 4b

1 Copy these and write the missing numbers.

1. 16 − 9 = ☐
2. 13 + ☐ = 16
3. ☐ + 37 = 127
4. 52 + ☐ = 89
5. 400 ÷ ☐ = 4
6. 50 + 70 + 30 = ☐
7. One quarter of 44
8. ☐ × 10 = 300
9. 19 + 18 = ☐

2 Draw three triangles to show the following:

1. an angle greater than a right angle
2. a right angle
3. two angles less than a right angle

3 Choose two digits from the circle to make this addition. Then find the answer.

2 ☐ + 5 ☐

Do this five times.

2 6 + 5 8 = 84

Circle contains: 6, 7, 8, 9

4 Choose a number from each box.
Make a subtraction and write down the answer.

47 69 56 88 79

31 22 15

Do this five times.

5
1. Add 10 to each of these numbers.

   74 91 193 1 452 300

2. Add 100 to each of these numbers.

   20 904 7 99 890 100

Practice 5a

1 Copy these and complete them.

1. $3 \times 5 =$ ___
2. $24 + 26 =$ ___
3. $8 \times 100 =$ ___
4. $400 \div 10 =$ ___
5. $75 + 75 =$ ___
6. 16 divided by 4
7. $76 - 23 =$ ___
8. $204 - 10 =$ ___
9. $93 + 10 =$ ___

2 Find the numbers hiding behind the stars.

1. ☆ $+ 3 = 17$
2. ☆ $+ 10 = 50$
3. ☆ $- 6 = 4$
4. ☆ $- 60 = 20$
5. ☆ $\times 3 = 6$
6. ☆ $\div 2 = 5$

3

1. Jane has 37 stickers. She buys 20 more. How many has she now?
2. Rodney counts 200 fingers in his class. How many children are there in the class?
3. How many feet have 25 children altogether?

4 Use the three digits in the first circle to make a number. Choose one digit in the second circle. Add it to your first number. Do this four times.

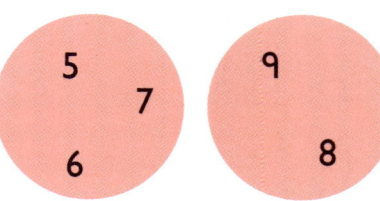

657 + 9 =

Circle 1: 5, 7, 6
Circle 2: 9, 8

5 Copy these and complete them.

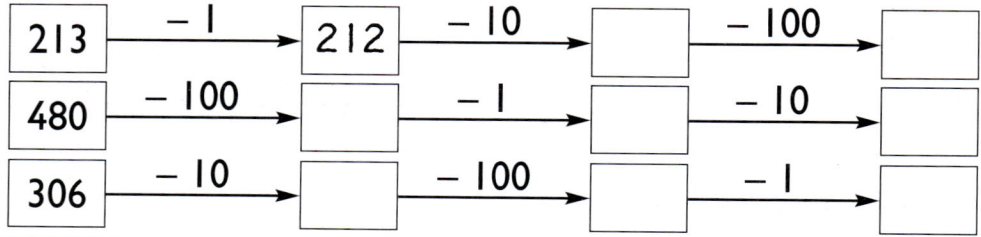

213 → −1 → 212 → −10 → ☐ → −100 → ☐
480 → −100 → ☐ → −1 → ☐ → −10 → ☐
306 → −10 → ☐ → −100 → ☐ → −1 → ☐

Practice 5b

1 Copy these and write the missing numbers.

1. 8 + ☐ = 17
2. ☐ − 11 = 9
3. ☐ × 6 = 24
4. 27 ÷ 3 = ☐
5. ☐ + 3 = 285
6. 300 + ☐ = 373
7. One tenth of ☐ = 10
8. 13 − ☐ = 5
9. 52 − ☐ = 46

2 Write these amounts in pounds and pence.

> 146p = £1.46

1. 146p
2. 250p
3. 400p
4. 603p
5. 7240p
6. 1000p
7. 82p
8. 5p

3 Write down the pairs of quantities that are the same.

> 1 litre = 1000 ml

| 1·5 litres | 4·1 litres | 1 litre | 7·3 litres | 3 litres | 0·3 litres |

| 4100 ml | 1000 ml | 1500 ml | 3000 ml | 300 ml | 7300 ml |

4 Copy these division grids and fill them in.

÷	10	20
2		10
5	2	

÷	12	36
3		
4		

÷	18	24
2		
3		

÷	30	60
5		
6		

÷	16	28
4		
2		

5 Use the digits 5, 6, 7 and 8 to complete this addition.
Then find the answer.

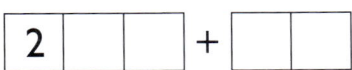

2 6 5 + 7 8 = 343

Do this three different ways.

Practice 6a

1 Copy these and complete them.

1. 120 − 60 = ___
2. Divide 35 by 5
3. 293 − 9 = ___
4. 315 + 11 = ___
5. Total of 18 and 19
6. Take 8 from 15
7. 150 − 60 = ___
8. 83 + 50 = ___
9. 127 − 40 = ___

2 How many millilitres of water are there in each jug?

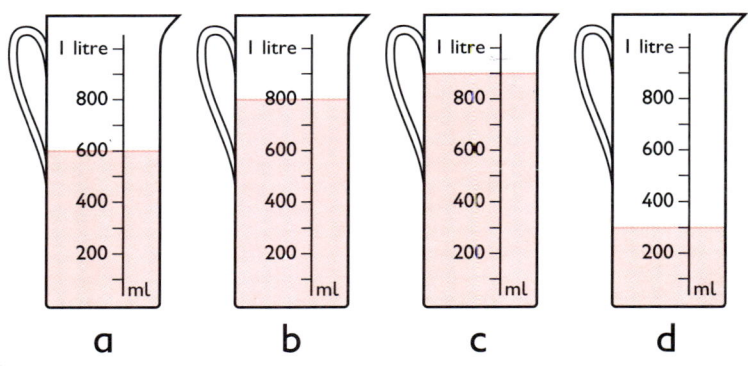

3 Write the cost of each item in pounds and pence.

231p 178p 200p 302p 1000p

4 Copy the sorting grid. Draw two angles in each column.

less than 1 right angle	equal to 1 right angle	more than 1 right angle

5 Copy these. Find the difference.

364, 359 → 6

1. 364, 359 →
2. 251, 242 →
3. 412, 407 →
4. 605, 595 →
5. 322, 318 →
6. 521, 515 →

Practice 6b

1 Copy these and write the missing numbers.

1. 19 − ☐ = 15
2. ☐ + 9 = 18
3. 460 + ☐ = 500
4. 45 + 29 = ☐
5. ☐ ÷ 2 = 20
6. 5 × 10 = ☐
7. Three quarters of 12
8. 45 + 46 = ☐
9. 82 − 59 = ☐

2

radio — £25   TV — £200   video recorder — £150

1. How much more than the video recorder does the TV cost?
2. How many radios could you buy for the price of one TV?
3. What is the total cost of the three items?

3 Copy these and complete them.

1. 251 − 8 = ___
2. 473 − 5 = ___
3. 326 − 19 = ___
4. 564 − 6 = ___
5. 142 − 7 = ___
6. 614 − 5 = ___

4 How many right angles are there in each shape?

1 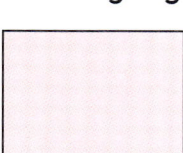   2 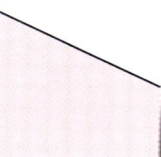   3 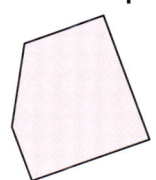   4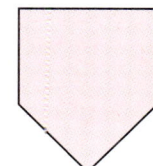

5 Use the four digits 4 5 6 7 to make the addition with the largest total.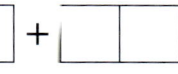

Use the same four digits to make the subtraction with the smallest difference.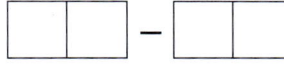

Practice 7a

1 Copy these and complete them.

1. 55 + 45 = ___
2. Multiply 8 by 5
3. 24 ÷ 4 = ___
4. 5 × 9 = ___
5. Double 65
6. 30 × 10 = ___
7. 900 ÷ 100 = ___
8. Half of 34
9. 5 × 100 = ___

2 Choose a hundreds digit and a tens digit. Make a 3- or 4-digit number with these, combined with any ones digit or thousands digit. Do five more.

hundreds
4   7
1

tens
1   4   7

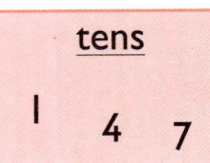

415
2170

3 Copy the patterns and fill in the numbers.

1. 2 + 2 = 4 → 20 + 20 = ☐ → 200 + 200 = ☐
2. 3 + 3 = ☐ → 30 + 30 = ☐ → 300 + 300 = ☐
3. 7 + 7 = ☐ → ☐ + ☐ = ☐ → ☐ + ☐ = ☐
4. 5 + 5 = ☐ → ☐ + ☐ = ☐ → ☐ + ☐ = ☐

4 Choose a number from each rectangle to make an addition. Write down the answer.

| 3000   800   6000   9004 |

| 7   5   2 |

3000 + 7 = 3007

Do this eight times.

5 Copy this subtraction and complete it.

| 4 | 0 | ☐ | − | 3 | ☐ | ☐ | = 7 |

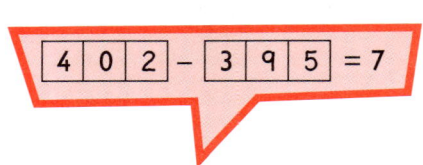

402 − 395 = 7

Find five different ways of doing this.

Practice 7b

1 Copy these and write the missing numbers.

1. $3 \times 8 = \square$
2. $32 \div 4 = \square$
3. $509 - \square = 499$
4. $\square + 2 + 7 = 22$
5. $35 \times \square = 70$
6. $\square + 50 = 130$
7. $\square \div 2 = 30$
8. $20 \times 5 = \square$
9. $40 \times \square = 80$

2 Copy these and fill in the missing numbers.

In any one addition, the missing numbers are the same.

$3 + 3 = 6$
$\square + \square = 60$
$\square + \square = 600$

$7 + 7 = 14$
$\square + \square = 140$
$\square + \square = 1400$

$12 + 12 = 24$
$\square + \square = 240$
$\square + \square = 2400$

3 Copy these and write the signs (+, −, ×, ÷) hiding behind the stars.

1. $7 ☆ 3 = 20 ☆ 2$
2. $15 ☆ 9 = 2 ☆ 3$
3. $6 ☆ 4 = 12 ☆ 12$
4. $5 ☆ 7 = 70 ☆ 35$

4 Use one of each of the digits $\boxed{4\ 3\ 0\ 7}$ to make a 4-digit number. Repeat until you have six 4-digit numbers.

Write each number like this:
3 thousands, 4 hundreds, 0 tens and 7 ones = 3407.

5 Copy these and fill in the missing numbers.

$2 + 5 = \square$
$7 - 2 = \square$

$20 + 50 = \square$
$70 - 20 = \square$

$200 + 500 = \square$
$700 - 200 = \square$

Carry on the pattern for two more boxes.

Practice 8a

1 Copy these and complete them.

1. 8 plus 4 plus 7 = ____
2. 30 less than 100
3. 37 + 73 = ____
4. 17 more than 100
5. Half of 600
6. 400 + 900 = ____
7. One tenth of 50
8. 80 + 70 = ____
9. 946 − 100 = ____

2 Copy these addition grids and complete them.

+	4	5
13		
15		

+	7	8
9		
6		

+		4
	12	
12		15

+		2
	17	13
9		

+		
	15	11
	18	14

3 Copy the grids and join numbers that differ by 100.

111	404	250	39	858	537	700
600	758	437	350	211	504	139

4 Add each pair of numbers. Write the addition and the answer.

1. 48, 93
2. 27, 56
3. 230, 480
4. 76, 114
5. 36, 128
6. 510, 640

5 Copy these and complete them.

1. 23 + 23 = ☐ → 23 + 24 = ☐
2. 46 + 46 = ☐ → 46 + 45 = ☐
3. 38 + 38 = ☐ → 37 + 39 = ☐
4. 190 + 190 = ☐ → 180 + 190 = ☐

Using doubles may help you.

Practice 8b

1 Copy these and write the missing numbers.

1. $10 \times 6 = \square$
2. $\square \div 2 = 20$
3. $\square + 400 = 1000$
4. $35 + \square = 100$
5. $\frac{1}{10}$ of $100 = \square$
6. $34 + 39 = \square$
7. $403 - 395 = \square$
8. $1004 - 997 = \square$
9. $31 \times 3 = \square$

2 Some of these additions are wrong. Check each by doing a subtraction.

1. $17 + 9 = 25$
2. $24 + 18 = 31$
3. $33 + 29 = 62$
4. $19 + 45 = 63$

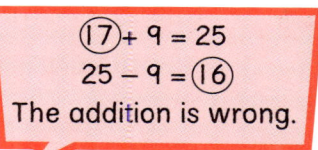
⑰ $+ 9 = 25$
$25 - 9 = $ ⑯
The addition is wrong.

3 Copy the subtraction grids and complete them.

−	17	12
8		
11		

−	15	19
14		
7		

−	13	
9		7
		1

−	18	
12	8	
		2

−		
	8	16
	6	14

4

1. Use the digits 5 1 9 6 to make five additions like this. Find the answers.

   $\square\square\square + \square$

   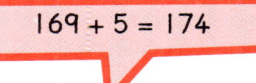
   $169 + 5 = 174$

2. Use the digits 4 7 8 2 3 to make five additions like this. Find the answers.

   $\square\square\square\square + \square$

   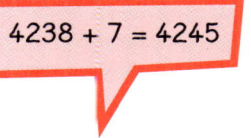
   $4238 + 7 = 4245$

5 Copy these triangles and find the pattern. Fill in the missing numbers.

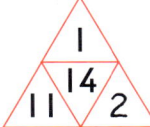
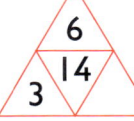
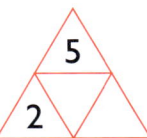

Numeracy Focus 4: Practice Book

Practice 9a

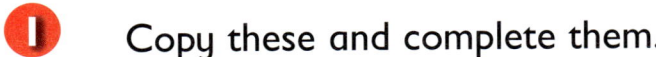

1 Copy these and complete them.

1. Double 12
2. 12 ÷ 2 = ___
3. 3 × 1 = ___
4. 13 + 14 = ___
5. 24 subtract 17
6. 30 + 90 = ___
7. Two eights
8. 75 × 2 = ___
9. 1 more than 3799

2 Choose a number from each box to make pairs of numbers with a difference of 6.

> 203, 197 → 6

| 203 | 701 | 402 | 505 | 604 |

| 499 | 197 | 695 | 598 | 396 |

3 Copy these and complete them.

1. 4079 —−3→ ☐
2. 863 —−7→ ☐
3. 2904 —−6→ ☐
4. 3285 —−9→ ☐
5. 511 —−8→ ☐
6. 721 —−5→ ☐

4 Check by adding. Which are wrong?

1. 62 − 19 = 53
2. 43 − 28 = 15
3. 75 − 36 = 39
4. 84 − 57 = 37

> ⓒ62 − 19 = 53
> ↓
> 53 + 19 = ⓒ72
> The subtraction is wrong.

5 Use the subtraction in the centre to find more subtractions.

Centre: 6 − 2 = 4

Top right: 60 − 20 = 40

Bottom right: 7 − 3 = 4

Make up four diagrams of your own.

Numeracy Focus 4: Practice Book

Practice 9b

1 Copy these and write the missing numbers.

1. 27 + ☐ = 52
2. 1099 + ☐ = 1100
3. 12 − 3 = ☐
4. ☐ − 396 = 5
5. ☐ − 1997 = 5
6. 6 × 5 = ☐
7. 47 + ☐ = 100
8. 16 ÷ 2 = ☐
9. ☐ × 7 = 14

2 Copy the grids and join pairs of numbers that have a difference of 1000.

1224	1424	1443	1234	1334	1324
2443	2224	2424	2234	2324	2334

3 Find the difference between the pairs of numbers.

Counting on or back may help.

1. 37, 41
2. 58, 64
3. 33, 29
4. 88, 79
5. 44, 52
6. 75, 66
7. 97, 102
8. 196, 201

4 Copy the sentence. Choose a number from each square to complete it.

☐ metres = ☐ centimetres = ☐ millimetres

Do this four more times.

| 2000 5000 7000 3000 8000 | 7 2 8 3 5 | 800 500 200 700 300 |

5 Copy the grid.

Make each row and each column total 20.

Do it again with different numbers.

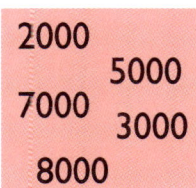

Practice 10a

1 Copy these and complete them.

1. 6 + 8 = ____
2. 987 + 6 = ____
3. 24 ÷ 3 = ____
4. 4 × 2 = ____
5. 43 – 37 = ____
6. 1 less than 7000
7. 370 add 30
8. 1700 – 800 = ____
9. One half of 80

2 Copy the diagram. Find the difference between the two numbers in each large triangle. Write the answer in the empty space.

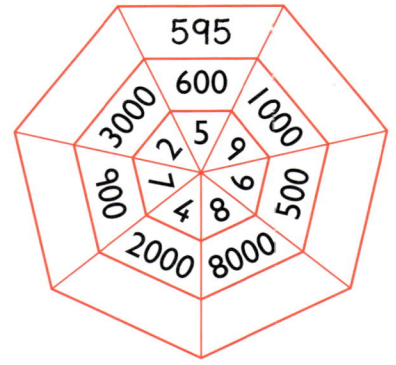

3 Copy the sorting grid. Draw three different polygons in each set.

3 straight sides	4 straight sides	5 straight sides

4 Copy these and complete them.

1. 5280 —– 1000 → 4280 —– 1000 → 3280 —– 1000 → ☐ —– 1000 → ☐
2. 9025 —– 1000 → ☐ —– 1000 → ☐ —– 1000 → ☐ —– 1000 → ☐
3. 6147 —– 1000 → ☐ —– 1000 → ☐ —– 1000 → ☐ —– 1000 → ☐

5 Make ten subtractions with 8 as the answer.

Practice 10b

1 Copy these and write the missing numbers.

1. ☐ + 500 = 800
2. 28 − 19 = ☐
3. 1 × ☐ = 10
4. 17 − 8 = ☐
5. 23 − ☐ = 6
6. 21 ÷ 3 = ☐
7. 5 × 6 = ☐
8. 17 + 50 − 50 = ☐
9. Double ☐ = 160

2 Do each of these twice. Use a different method each time.

1. 26 + 37
2. 84 − 17
3. 52 + 16
4. 45 − 28
5. 23 + 68
6. 93 − 75

3 Choose your own digits to complete the subtractions.

1. 4☐☐ − 3☐☐ = 7
2. 8☐☐☐ − 7☐☐☐ = 5
3. 6☐☐ − 5☐☐ = 2
4. 9☐☐☐ − 8☐☐☐ = 8

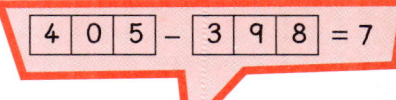
405 − 398 = 7

4 Choose a number from each rectangle and find the difference.

142   503   7106   8495

7   8   9   6

Do this eight times.

5 Make up ten amounts of money using a £1 coin and four other coins.

Practice 11a

1 Copy these and complete them.

1. 16 − 7 = ___
2. 52 take away 35
3. 23 + 25 = ___
4. 72 − 69 = ___
5. 10 more than 5992
6. 2 × 0 = ___
7. Double 17
8. Add 29 to 82
9. 415 + 7 = ___

2 Copy these and draw the lines of symmetry.

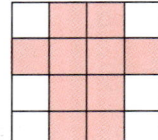 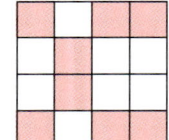 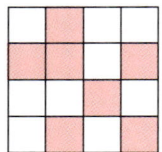 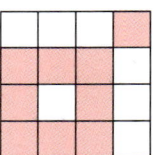

3 A metre ruler is 100 cm long. Write which of these is longer than 1 metre, about 1 metre, shorter than 1 metre.

1. height of a desk
2. width of a door
3. length of your foot
4. length of your arm
5. your height
6. length of a car
7. length of your stride
8. length of your leg
9. round your waist

4 Copy these sequences. What numbers are hiding behind the stars?

1. 15 19 23 ☆ ☆ ☆ ☆ ☆
2. 8 14 20 ☆ ☆ ☆ ☆ ☆
3. 10 17 24 ☆ ☆ ☆ ☆ ☆

5 Use the digits in the circle to make two 3-digit numbers between 100 and 200.

Write all the odd numbers that are between your two numbers.

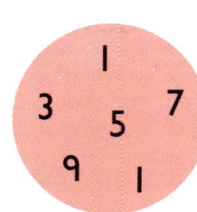

Numeracy Focus 4: Practice Book

Practice 11b

L. 21/06

1 Copy these and write the missing numbers.

1. 73 − ☐ = 40
2. 9090 + ☐ = 9100
3. ☐ + 18 = 35
4. 500 + ☐ = 1100
5. 3 × ☐ = 15
6. 6 + 9 = ☐
7. ☐ − 8 = 5996
8. 5 × 8 = ☐
9. 27 ÷ 3 = ☐

2 Write the pairs of equal length.

$\frac{3}{4}$ m	$\frac{1}{2}$ m	$\frac{1}{4}$ m	$\frac{1}{10}$ m	$\frac{1}{2}$ km	$\frac{3}{4}$ km	$\frac{1}{4}$ km
750 m	500 m	750 mm	500 mm	100 mm	250 mm	250 m

3 Copy these number jumps and complete them.

+100 +100 +100 +100 +100 +100 +100 +100

37   137

+100 +100 +100 +100 +100 +100 +100 +100

904

4
1. How many 20p coins make £5?
2. How many 2p coins make £2?
3. How many 5p coins make £4?
4. How many 50p coins make £10?

5 Copy these shapes.
Write down everything you know about each shape.

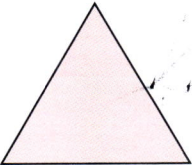  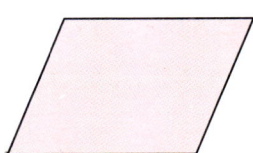 

Practice 12a

1 Copy these and complete them.

1. 11 − 9 = ___
2. 542 + 50 = ___
3. 90 + 70 = ___
4. Multiply 7 by 4
5. 18 ÷ 2 = ___
6. 3597 add 8
7. Double 65
8. 2 times 6
9. 3004 − 2996 = ___

2 Copy these sequences. What numbers are hiding behind the stars?

1. 18 15 12 ☆ ☆ ☆ ☆
2. 32 27 22 ☆ ☆ ☆ ☆
3. 50 42 34 ☆ ☆ ☆ ☆

3 Copy these diagrams. Write the sum in the top triangle and the difference in the bottom triangle.

3 ⋈ 15 (18 top, 12 bottom)   9 ⋈ 15   20 ⋈ 80   14 ⋈ 26   35 ⋈ 65

4 Copy these and find the answers.

20 + 21	17 + 18	34 + 35
21 + 22	18 + 19	35 + 36
22 + 23	19 + 20	36 + 37

Look for patterns

Write about any patterns you find.

5 Arrange the numbers 10 20 30 40 in the circles in as many ways as you can.

○—○—○—○

20—10—40—30

Order your sets of four numbers in some way.

Practice 12b

1 Copy these and write the missing numbers.

1. 2 × 8 = ☐
2. 69 + 18 = ☐
3. ☐ + 6 = 391
4. 16 − 4 = ☐
5. ☐ + 51 = 100
6. ☐ − 20 = 85
7. 4907 + ☐ = 5007
8. Double ☐ = 16
9. 80 + ☐ = 130

2 Copy the grids and the shaded shapes.

Draw the reflections of the shapes in the mirror lines.

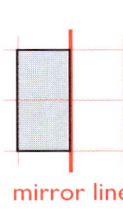
1
mirror line

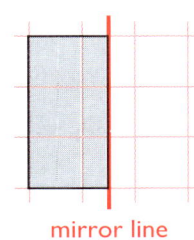
2
mirror line

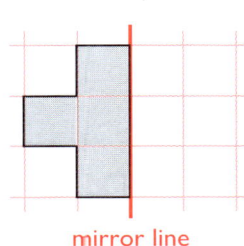
3
mirror line

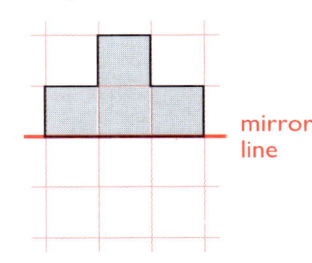
4
mirror line

3

1 Measure this pencil. Write its length in centimetres.

2 How many millimetres long is the pencil?

4 Write two examples for each of these statements.

1. The sum of two even numbers is an even number.
2. The difference between two odd numbers is an even number.
3. A multiple of 5 can be either even or odd.

Numeracy Focus 4: Practice Book

Practice 13a

1 Copy these and complete them.

1. 7 add 5
2. 59 + 61 = ___
3. Take 8 from 91
4. 170 − 90 = ___
5. 170 ÷ 2 = ___
6. Five times nine
7. 10 less than 2305
8. The sum of 500 and 26
9. 500 − 9 = ___

2 Copy these multiplication grids and complete them.

×	2	5	4
8			
3			

×	3	10	4
9			
5			

×		3	
2	8		
			40

×		4	2
		35	14
6			

3
1. Sam has 45 stickers. He buys 50 more. How many has he altogether?
2. A bus has 52 passengers then 37 get off. How many are left on the bus?
3. There are 8 choc-ices in a box. How many are there in 5 boxes?
4. Theresa has 10 sweets. She gives half to Sue. How many has she left?

4 Copy this 3 × 6 grid.
How many squares are in each row?
How many squares are in each column?
How many squares are there altogether?
Do this for these grids:
2 × 5   4 × 3   6 × 4   3 × 7

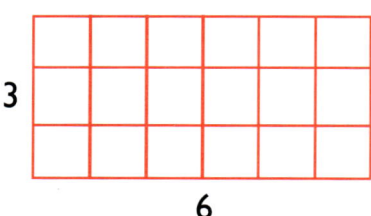

5 Copy and complete this. What do you notice?

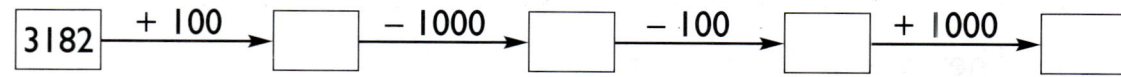

Try this with six more numbers greater than 2000.

Numeracy Focus 4: Practice Book

Practice 13b

L. 05/07

1 Copy these and write the missing numbers.

1 7 + 8 = ☐
2 20 ÷ 4 = ☐
3 ☐ × 0 = 0
4 ☐ + 351 = 700
5 392 − ☐ = 342
6 222 − ☐ = 215
7 500 − ☐ = 350
8 6 × 4 = ☐
9 ☐ ÷ 2 = 95

2 Draw these shapes.

1 a semi-circle
2 a 3-sided polygon with all sides different lengths
3 a 4-sided polygon with all its sides equal
4 a 5-sided polygon with two right angles

3 Copy these multiplication grids and complete them.

×	2	3	4
9			
6			

×	2	5	10
5			
8			

×	4		
	12		21
5		40	

×			
	30	20	70
	9	6	21

4 Shaun has a rule. To multiply by 5, he multiplies by 10 and halves the answer.

Use Shaun's rule to do these.

1 24 × 5
2 86 × 5
3 262 × 5

5 I am thinking of two numbers. What are my two numbers?

1 They are both odd and between 359 and 370.
2 They are both even and differ by 156.
3 One is odd, the other is even and their sum is 201.

Numeracy Focus 4: Practice Book

Practice 14a

1 Copy these and complete them.

1. 23 + 23 = ___
2. 100 more than 6940
3. 51 plus 49
4. 50 + 80 = ___
5. 3 times 8
6. 94 − 88 = ___
7. 119 + 120 = ___
8. 16 ÷ 4 = ___
9. 7000 − 4 = ___

2 Copy these and write the numbers that are hiding behind stars.

1. 30 × 7 = ☆
   7 × ☆ = 210
2. 6 × 40 = ☆
   40 × ☆ = 240
3. 90 × ☆ = 450
   ☆ × 5 = 450

3 Choose two numbers from the box to make a fraction which is less than 1. Write it down in figures and words.

Do this for six more fractions.

| 1 | 2 | 3 | 4 | 10 |

½   one half

4 Copy these and find the answers.

| 1 + 2 + 3 = ___ | 4 + 5 + 6 = ___ | 9 + 10 + 11 = ___ |
| 3 × 2 = ___ | 3 × 5 = ___ | 3 × 10 = ___ |

Make up six more like these.

5 Copy and complete these.

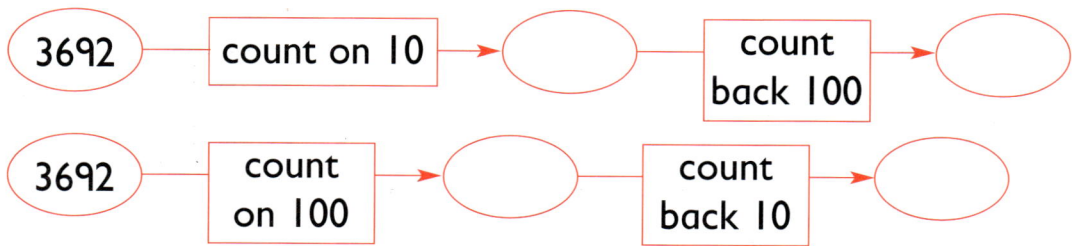

Do this six more times, choosing different start numbers.

Practice 14b

1 Copy these and write the missing numbers.

1. $36 \div 4 = \square$
2. $3 \times 5 = \square$
3. $140 + \square = 270$
4. $\square + 8 = 6415$
5. $15 - 7 = \square$
6. $\square + 52 = 60$
7. $\square + 1000 = 8888$
8. $\square - 260 = 400$
9. $\square \times 7 = 35$

2 Copy this grid. For each number, write its double above and its half below.

double	20								
number	10	50	14	20	32	46	180	370	2600
half	5								

3 What fraction of each shape is shaded?
What fraction of each shape is not shaded?

1    2 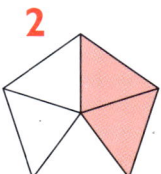   3 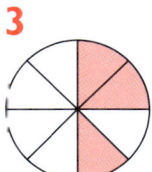   4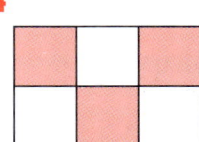

4 A large tin of dog food lasts 3 days and a small tin lasts 2 days.

1. How many days will 4 large tins last?
2. How many days will 2 large and 3 small tins last altogether?
3. How many large and small tins are needed for exactly 13 days?

5 Choose your own digits to complete these subtractions.

1. $4\square - 3\square = 5$
2. $4\square\square - 3\square\square = 55$
3. $4\square\square\square - 3\square\square\square = 555$

Do this three more times.

Practice 15a

1 Copy these and complete them.

1. 15 minus 9
2. 680 + 700 = ___
3. 3 times 6
4. 24 ÷ 4 = ___
5. 304 − 8 = ___
6. Subtract 200 from 350
7. 6 multiplied by 3
8. 46 + 58 = ___
9. 310 − 60 = ___

2 Copy the grid and fill in the missing numbers.

number	12	24	36	60	120	600
one half is	6					
one quarter is	3					
one third is	4					

3 Copy these sentences and complete them.

1. Multiples of 10 end in ___.
2. Multiples of 2 end in 0, 2, ___, ___ or ___.
3. Multiples of 5 end in ___ or ___.

4
1. What is the third month of the year?
2. What time does this clock show?
3. What time is it 3 hours after noon?
4. How many more days are there in July than in June?

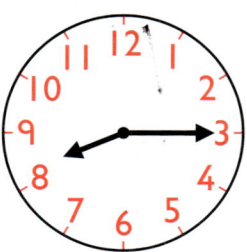

5
1. Write two fractions that are equal to $\frac{1}{2}$.
2. Write two fractions that are equal to $\frac{1}{4}$.

Numeracy Focus 4: Practice Book

Practice 15b

L. 26/08

1 Copy these and write the missing numbers.

1. 20 ÷ 5 = ☐
2. 210 − ☐ = 400
3. 8 + 6 = ☐
4. 4 × 7 = ☐
5. ☐ − 5 = 4439
6. Half of ☐ = 26
7. ☐ + 80 = 123
8. 89 − ☐ = 22
9. ☐ + 37 = 69

2 Copy these and find the answers. What do you notice?

| 2 × 4 | 2 × 11 | 2 × 20 | 2 × 43 | 2 × 150 |
| double 4 | double 11 | double 20 | double 43 | double 150 |

3 In each grid, all the numbers can be divided exactly by the same number. Write down this number.

25	15	50
30	20	45

8	20	12
18	6	24

12	24	36
18	27	15

50	70	20
40	90	60

4

hopper £3.99

pogo stick £10.99

trampoline £34.99

1. How much does Aliyah pay for a hopper and a pogo stick?
2. How much more is the trampoline than the pogo stick?
3. How much does Leo pay for two hoppers?

5 Make £1.50 with three coins.

Make £1.50 with four, five and then six coins.

Practice 16a

Emily 03/02
D. 10/02
Lak 02/9/10

1 Copy these and complete them.

1. 249 + 251 = ___
2. 3 × 9 = ___
3. Add 66 and 77
4. 110 less than 200
5. Double 29
6. 305 − 299 = ___
7. Multiply 4 by 5
8. 506 − 9 = ___
9. 826 + 9 = ___

2

1. In a 400 metre race Saul has run 150 metres. How many metres has he left to run?
2. A kettle holds 1500 ml and a jug holds 500 ml. How many full jugs are needed to fill the kettle?
3. A jar of jam weighs 450 grams. How many grams do 2 jars weigh?

3 This is a tally chart of colours that children in a class like best.

1. How many children like green best?
2. How many like blue best?
3. How many children are there in the class?

red	⊞ I
green	III
blue	⊞ ⊞ II
yellow	⊞ III

4 Choose one fraction from each circle to make a pair with a total of 1.

Make five more pairs.

Circle 1: $\frac{1}{4}$, $\frac{3}{10}$, $\frac{1}{2}$, $\frac{3}{4}$, $\frac{1}{3}$, $\frac{5}{8}$

Circle 2: $\frac{1}{4}$, $\frac{3}{4}$, $\frac{3}{8}$, $\frac{2}{3}$, $\frac{1}{2}$, $\frac{7}{10}$

$\frac{1}{2}, \frac{1}{2} \rightarrow 1$

5 Choose words from the oval to complete this number.

___ thousand ___ hundred and ___

Write the number in figures.

Do this five times.

one thousand three hundred and nine
1309

three, twenty, one, eighty, nine, forty

Practice 16b

1 Copy these and write the missing numbers.

1. $57 - \square = 9$
2. $\square \times 1 = 57$
3. $\square + 17 = 304$
4. $14 - 9 = \square$
5. Double $\square = 62$
6. $6090 - \square = 6089$
7. $\square - 7995 = 6$
8. $100 \div \square = 50$
9. $4 \times 3 = \square$

2 What time is it?

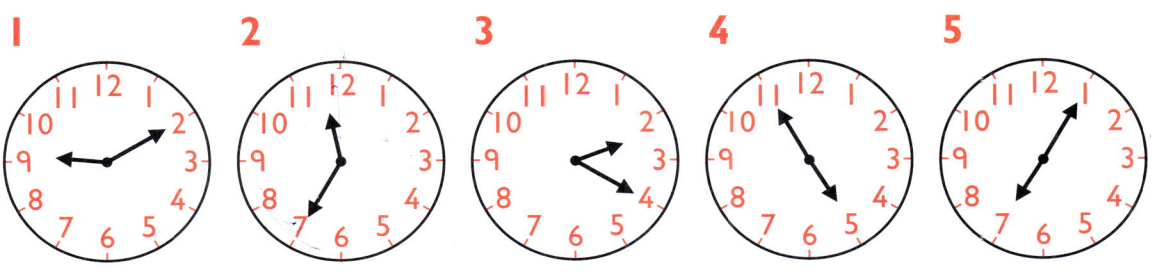

3
1. How many metres are there in 2 kilometres?
2. What fraction of a litre is 500 millilitres?
3. Write 2500 grams in kilograms.
4. How much longer than 500 millimetres is 2 metres?

4 Greg says he can see the polygons a, b and c in this large triangle.

How many of each kind of polygon can you see in the large triangle?

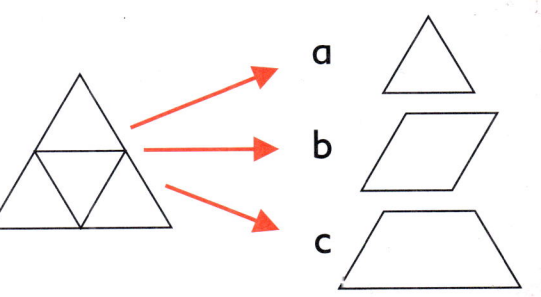

5 Use the numbers $\boxed{28 \quad 53 \quad 81 \quad 134 \quad 162}$ to make as many different addition or subtraction sentences as you can.

Practice 17a

1 Copy these and complete them.

1 8 + 7 = ___	2 Increase 78 by 40	3 10 multiplied by 6
4 80 × 2 = ___	5 2004 – 7 = ___	6 100 less than 8050
7 5 × 7 = ___	8 15 ÷ 5 = ___	9 66 add 32

2 Copy this grid.
Multiply each number by 10, write the answer in the top row.
Divide each number by 10, write the answer in the bottom row.

× 10	700						
number	70	20	500	60	40	900	80
÷ 10	7						

3 Write these times using a.m. or p.m.

1 after midday
2 before midday
3 before midday
4 after midday

4 Alim has 45 stickers. Helena has twice as many as Alim.
Lena has 55 more than Alim. Rowan has 18 less than Alim.
How many stickers do Helena, Lena and Rowan each have?

5 Choose digits from the circle to make this addition.
Find the answer.

☐ 0 0 + ☐ 0 0

Do this six times.

Practice 17b

1 Copy these and write the missing numbers.

1. ☐ × 10 = 90
2. 9 + 8 = ☐
3. Half of ☐ = 78
4. 3 × 7 = ☐
5. ☐ − 2 = 4998
6. ☐ − 200 = 739
7. 35 × ☐ = 70
8. ☐ ÷ 2 = 140
9. ☐ − 8 = 67

2 Some children made a bar chart of the colours they liked best.

1. Which colour did only one child like best?
2. How many more children liked green than liked blue?
3. Which colour was liked by twice as many children as liked green?

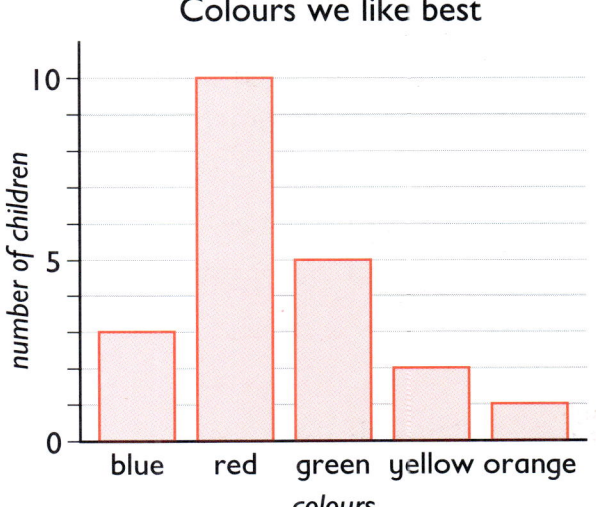

Colours we like best

3 Estimate to the nearest ten the numbers to which the arrows are pointing.

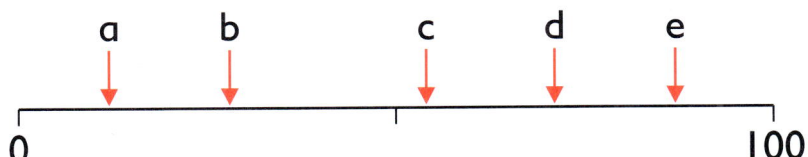

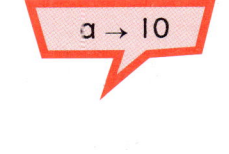

a → 10

4 Make up five questions about this bus timetable.

	London	Watford	Leicester	Leeds	Newcastle	Edinburgh
arrive		2:40	4:30	6:50	9:05	11:45
depart	1:30	2:55	5:00	7:05	9:47	

Numeracy Focus 4: Practice Book

Practice 18a

1 Copy these and complete them.

1. One half of 50
2. 2 × 9 = ___
3. 4 × 6 = ___
4. 240 add 230
5. 601 − 594 = ___
6. 100 minus 64
7. 3333 + 1000 = ___
8. Double 300
9. 2432 − 7 = ___

2 Choose a number from each circle so that their sum is a multiple of 3. Find ten such pairs.

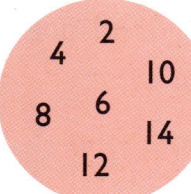 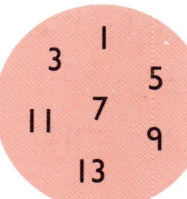 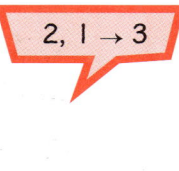

3 Copy the grids. In each empty box, write a number that can be rounded to the nearest 10 to give the number in the centre.

(Grid 1: 277 top-left; 280, 276 middle; 283 bottom)
(Grid 2: centre 110)
(Grid 3: centre 500)
(Grid 4: centre 450)

4 Some of these calculations are correct, some are not correct. Check by doing the inverse operation.

1. 37 + 65 = 112
2. 78 + 84 = 162
3. 156 − 97 = 69
4. 274 − 39 = 242

(speech bubble: ㊲ + 65 = 112 / 112 − 65 = ㊼ / not correct)

5 Copy these two subtractions, choose a digit from the circle and write it in each empty box. Work out the answers.

(speech bubble: 500 − 5 = 495 / 50 − 5 = 45)

☐ 0 0 − ☐ = ▨   ☐ 0 − ☐ = ▨

Do this six times.

Practice 18b

1 Copy these and write the missing numbers.

1. $3002 - \square = 2992$
2. Double $\square = 4000$
3. $13 - 5 = \square$
4. $25 \div 5 = \square$
5. $\frac{1}{2}$ of $\square = 37$
6. $505 - \square = 9$
7. $24 + \square = 60$
8. $21 + \square = 41$
9. $180 \div \square = 90$

2 Choose a number from each oval to make an addition and then a subtraction.

Do this six times.

130 160
110 100

20 70
60 90

> $130 + 20 = 150$
> $130 - 20 = 110$

3 Multiply each number in the box by 100.

29   137   4   60   528   100   10   701

4
1. How many more candles are there in the large box than in the small box?
2. Melissa buys three small boxes. How many candles does she get? How much do they cost her?
3. How many times as many candles are there in the large box as in the small box?
4. Dylan buys one large box of candles. Astrid buys 4 small boxes. How much more does Astrid pay?

12 CANDLES 99p

48 CANDLES £3.50

5 Choose two numbers to make this sentence true.

Double $\square$ = half of $\square$.

Do this six times.

Numeracy Focus 4: Practice Book

Practice 19a

1 Copy these and complete them.

1. 14 − 6 = ___
2. 100 ÷ 2 = ___
3. One quarter of 800
4. Three sevens
5. Decrease 400 by 230
6. 140 − 80 = ___
7. 694 + 8 = ___
8. 4070 − 1000 = ___
9. 460 add 440

2 Adding a multiple of 10 and then adjusting will help you do these.

> 24 + 89 = 24 + 90 − 1

1. 24 + 89 = ___
2. 36 + 78 = ___
3. 65 + 97 = ___
4. 59 + 26 = ___
5. 45 + 69 = ___
6. 77 + 58 = ___

3

1. Jack takes a car journey 476 miles long. How many miles are left to travel when he has gone 150 miles?
2. There are 172 boys and 228 girls in a school. How many children are there in the school?
3. A bus has 37 passengers upstairs and 45 downstairs. How many passengers are there on the bus?

4 Find two numbers from the grid that total 1000.

Do this eight times.

300	250	850	350
800	900	450	600
650	100	700	150
550	750	400	200

> 300, 700 → 1000

5 Draw a number line 12 cm long. Mark it from 0 to 1. Put a cross on the line to mark $\frac{1}{4}$. Choose four fractions of your own and mark them on the line.

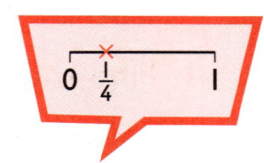

Practice 19b

1 Copy these and write the missing numbers.

1. Double ☐ = 90
2. 2 × 7 = ☐
3. ¼ of ☐ = 20
4. 6059 − ☐ = 3059
5. 270 − ☐ = 200
6. Half of ☐ = 420
7. ☐ × 2 = 280
8. 39 + 39 = ☐
9. 3 × ☐ = 60

2 Copy the numbers. Match each pair of numbers which have a sum of 100.

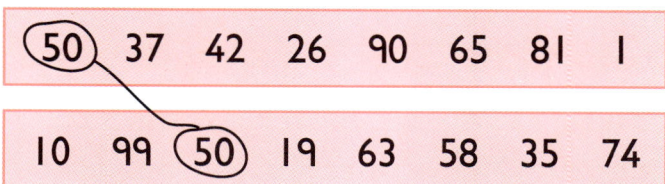

3 Copy these and complete them.

> 53 − 28 =
> 53 − 30 + 2

1. 53 − 28 = ☐
2. 42 − 17 = ☐
3. 74 − 46 = ☐
4. 66 − 39 = ☐
5. 88 − 29 = ☐
6. 47 − 38 = ☐

4 Choose a number from each circle to make an addition.

Do this six times.

> 5 + 36 + 55 =
> 55 + 5 + 36

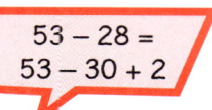

5 Write down two numbers that are next to each other in this grid.

Find their difference.

Do this for all 12 pairs of numbers that are next to each other.

> 155, 8 → 147

155	8	417
6	371	9
803	7	234

Practice 20a

1 Copy these and complete them.

1 58 − 29 = ___   2 510 + 490 = ___   3 83 add 50
4 Double 400   5 30 ÷ 5 = ___   6 One tenth of 60
7 457 − 30 = ___ 8 8003 − 7995 = ___ 9 36 plus 37

2 Copy this addition. Find the answer. 36 + 45 + 97 + 62

3
1 Faith swims from 9:30 a.m. to 10:15 a.m. How long does she swim?
2 A train leaves a station at 11:40 a.m. and arrives at its destination at 12:30 p.m. How long does the journey take?
3 Clyde's birthday is on 8th July and his sister's is on 8th August. How many days are there from Clyde's birthday to his sister's?

4

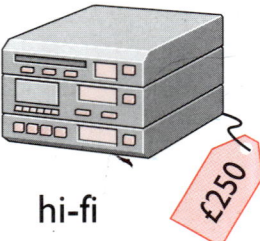
hi-fi £250

TV £470

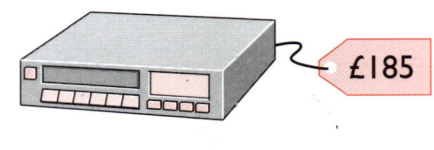
video recorder £185

1 How much more does the hi-fi cost than the video recorder?
2 What is the total cost of the three items?
3 Paul pays one tenth of the cost of the hi-fi as a deposit. How much is the deposit?

5 Choose numbers from the grid for each multiplication.

___ × ___ = 21   ___ × ___ = 60
___ × ___ = 45   ___ × ___ = 18
___ × ___ = 32   ___ × ___ = 28

2	3	4
5	6	7
8	9	10

Numeracy Focus 4: Practice Book

Practice 20b

1 Copy these and write the missing numbers.

1. ☐ − 85 = 100
2. $\frac{1}{5}$ of ☐ = 40
3. 615 × ☐ = 6150
4. 492 + ☐ = 501
5. 46 + 46 = ☐
6. 860 ÷ ☐ = 86
7. 700 × ☐ = 7000
8. 52 − ☐ = 5
9. 80 + ☐ = 130

2 Copy these and find the missing numbers.

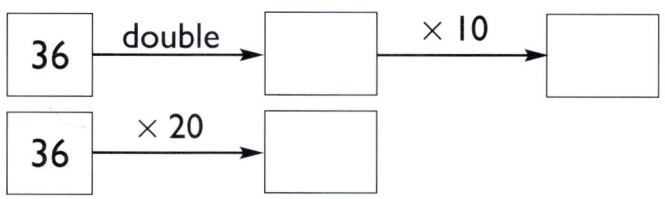

Do this four times, using a number from the box as your starting number.

| 17 | 42 | 59 | 130 | 250 |

3 Write down the six pairs of calculations which have the same answer.

27 + 81	double 29	27 × 4	311 − 289
16 × 5	146 + 24	580 ÷ 10	one half of 32
one half of 44	8000 ÷ 100	512 − 496	17 × 10

4 Copy these and write in the missing fractions.

☐ kg = 500 g   ☐ l = 250 ml   ☐ l = 750 ml
☐ kg = 200 g   ☐ kg = 250 g   ☐ l = 100 ml

5 Use three digits to complete this subtraction.

☐ 0 0 − ☐ 0 0 = 800

Find as many different answers as you can.

Practice 21a

1 Copy these and complete them.

1. 4 times 10
2. 9 plus 4
3. 800 − 6 = ___
4. One fifth of 70
5. 803 − 798 = ___
6. Add 700 to 800
7. 280 ÷ 2 = ___
8. 80 subtract 53
9. 5 × 4 = ___

2 Draw number lines for these additions.

1. 36 + 23
2. 42 + 17
3. 59 + 32
4. 28 + 64
5. 18 + 75
6. 53 + 49

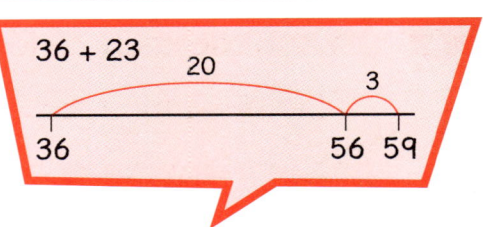

3 Choose the most sensible unit from the box, to measure these amounts.

1. an apple
2. a spoonful of cough medicine
3. a car
4. a lorry load of hay
5. lemonade in a large bottle
6. a small bottle of vinegar

| g | kg | l | ml |

4 Copy the two rectangles.
Match each 3D shape to a 2D shape that it has as a face.

| triangle | square | circle |

| cube | hemisphere | tetrahedron | cone | cylinder |

5 Use the digits in the circle to make a 3-digit number.
Multiply your number by 100.
Do this ten times.

5 9 0 3

Numeracy Focus 4: Practice Book

Practice 21b

1 Copy these and write the missing numbers.

1. $34 - 17 = \square$
2. $35 \div 5 = \square$
3. $\frac{1}{10}$ of $\square = 62$
4. $5055 - 4955 = \square$
5. $420 + \square = 1220$
6. Double $\square = 3400$
7. $80 \times \square = 160$
8. $5 \times 3 = \square$
9. $110 \div \square = 55$

2 Write down two numbers from the box.
Find the sum in two different ways.
Do this ten times.

| 58 | 317 | 26 | 84 | 609 | 438 |

3 Copy this chart. Fill in the numbers.

shape	number of quadrilateral faces	number of triangular faces	total number of faces
cuboid			
tetrahedron			
triangular prism			
square pyramid			

4 Copy these grids. Write in numbers so that the total of the four numbers in each grid is 20.

3	7
6	

	2
4	5

	3
8	

9	
6	

7	

	1

Practice 22a

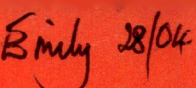

1 Copy these and complete them.

1. 800 add 400
2. 3 times 8
3. 80 + 60 = ___
4. One half of £1
5. 1 + 3 + 2 = ___
6. 17 × 10 = ___
7. Four sixes
8. 100 − 47 = ___
9. 48 + 19 = ___

2 Write down how much is on each scale.

1 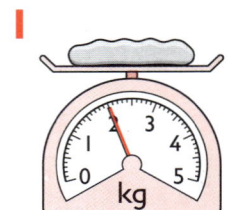 2 3  4  5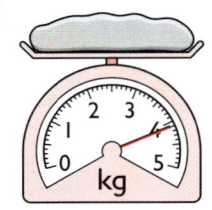

3 Copy the number of each net. From the box choose the name of the shape that each net makes. Write it next to the net number.

1 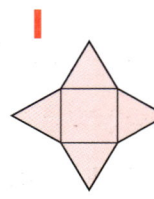 2  3  4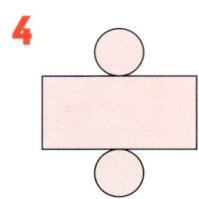

| cube | cuboid | cylinder | square | pyramid |

4
1. How many teabags are there in 10 boxes?
2. How much do 10 boxes cost?
3. How many kilograms do 10 boxes weigh?

5 Make four copies of this multiplication grid.

Complete your four grids using as many different numbers as you can.

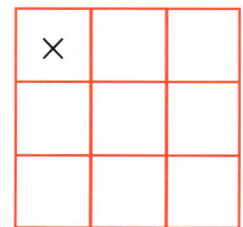

Numeracy Focus 4: Practice Book

Practice 22b

1 Copy these and write the missing numbers.

1. 110 − ☐ = 40
2. 2 + 3 + ☐ = 6
3. ☐ × 10 = 400
4. 36 + ☐ = 45
5. 4 + ☐ + 7 = 17
6. 72 − 36 = ☐
7. ☐ ÷ 10 = 405
8. one tenth of ☐ = 700
9. $\frac{1}{2}$ of ☐ = 50 cm

2 Choose two numbers from the box to complete this sentence.

☐ l = ☐ ml.

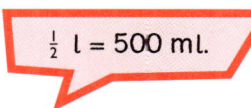
$\frac{1}{2}$ l = 500 mL.

| $\frac{1}{2}$ | 250 | 500 | $\frac{3}{4}$ | 2 | $\frac{1}{10}$ |
| 100 | 2000 | 3 | $\frac{1}{4}$ | 750 | 3000 |

Do this six times.

3
1. How much do five £1 and six 50p coins make altogether?
2. How much do ten £2 and ten £1 coins make altogether?
3. How much do twenty 20p and twenty £2 coins make altogether?
4. How much do fifty 10p and fifty 50p coins make altogether?

4 Copy these and write the signs that are hiding behind the stars.

1. 5 ☆ 2 ☆ 10 = 100
2. 23 ☆ 41 ☆ 36 = 100
3. 278 ☆ 22 ☆ 200 = 100
4. 124 ☆ 46 ☆ 70 = 100
5. 50 ☆ 4 ☆ 2 = 100
6. 400 ☆ 152 ☆ 148 = 100

5 Use the digits 6 7 8 to make this addition. Find the answer.

☐☐ + ☐9   Do this six times.

Why are there always two additions with the same answer?

Practice 23a

1 Copy these and complete them.

1	13 − 8 = ___	2	Take 70 from 350	3	One half of 26
4	47 + 53 = ___	5	4 + 5 + 6 = ___	6	600 add 400
7	700 ÷ 10 = ___	8	56 + 35 = ___	9	32 ÷ 4 = ___

2 Copy these and match amounts.

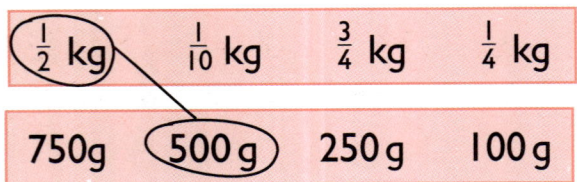

3 Copy these. Write temperatures to complete them.

1 −5 °C is colder than ___ .
2 −3 °C is warmer than ___ .
3 0 °C is warmer than ___ .
4 1 °C is colder than ___ .
5 ___ is colder than −7 °C.
6 ___ is warmer than −2 °C.

4 Copy this table. Find the 3D shapes which fit the numbers. Write their names in the table.

name	number of faces	number of vertices	number of edges
	5	6	9
	7	10	15
	6	6	10
	5	5	8

5 Copy the diagram. Write the numbers 1, 2, 3, 4, 5, 5, 6, 7, 8, 9 in the circles so that each row totals 25 and each column totals 10.

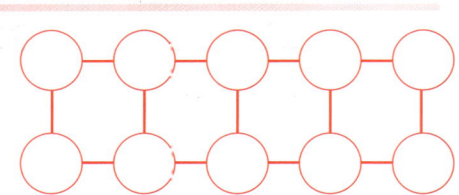

Numeracy Focus 4: Practice Book

Practice 23b

1 Copy these and write the missing numbers.

1. $3 \times \square = 30$
2. $\square + 5 - 5 = 19$
3. $\square - 19 = 28$
4. $70 + 70 = \square$
5. $\square + 28 = 57$
6. $283 + \square = 300$
7. $\frac{1}{4}$ of $\square = 50\,g$
8. $\square + 80 = 671$
9. $204 - \square = 8$

2 Change 1 number in each calculation to make them all correct.

$16 - 5 - 10 = 2$	$14 \times 2 \times 5 = 130$	$24 \div 2 \times 4 = 32$
$22 + 7 - 16 = 12$	$28 + 15 + 12 = 56$	$5 \times 6 \div 4 = 10$

3

1. There are 3 litres of water in a pan. 500 millilitres boils away. How much water is left in the pan?
2. Polly builds a tower 8 cylinders high. Each cylinder is 25 centimetres tall. How high is the tower?
3. Glen mixes 728 grams of baking apples with half a kilogram of sugar. How many grams is the mixture?

4 Write the number from the box for each arrow.

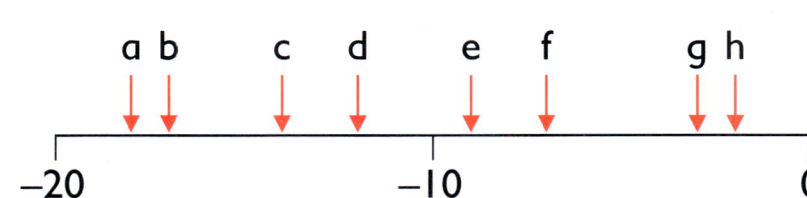
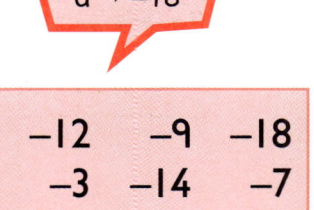

$a \rightarrow -18$

5 Copy and continue the patterns. Find the answers.

$30 + 10$	$30 - 10$	30×10	$30 \div 10$
$40 + 10$	$40 - 10$	40×10	$40 \div 10$

Numeracy Focus 4: Practice Book

Practice 24a

1 Copy these and complete them.

1. Add 188 to 19
2. Take 31 from 100
3. 8 + 2 + 7 = ___
4. One quarter of £1
5. 500 ÷ 10 = ___
6. 140 times 2
7. Double 40
8. 38 − 9 = ___
9. 4 × 9 = ___

2 Copy these and write the missing digits.

1. 3☐ + ☐7 = 96
2. 7☐ − ☐8 = 45
3. ☐5 + 6☐ = 81
4. ☐4 − 7☐ = 5
5. 4☐ + 2☐ = 72
6. 5☐ − 3☐ = 19

3 Use the numbers in the box to make ten multiplications. Find the answers.

> 5 × 7 = 35

| 5 | 6 | 7 | 8 | 9 | 30 | 42 | 56 | 72 |

4

1. Cory leaves home at 8:25 a.m. and arrives at school at 8:43 a.m. How long does she take to get to school?
2. On Thursday 27th March, Dai buys a ticket for a pop concert to be held 13 days later. When is the pop concert?
3. Year 4 leave on a school trip at 9:30. The journey takes 75 minutes. At what time do they arrive?

5 Copy each sentence three times. Use each integer in the box once only to complete the six sentences.

0	−7	−4
−5	+2	−8
−6	+1	−3
+3	−2	−1

___ is more than ___.

___ is less than ___.

Numeracy Focus 4: Practice Book

Practice 24b

1 Copy these and write the missing numbers.

1. ☐ × 100 = 1800
2. ☐ + 500 = 1200
3. 22 + ☐ = 93
4. 28 − ☐ = 19
5. 8 + 2 + ☐ = 16
6. 11 + ☐ + 8 = 28
7. ☐ ÷ 10 = 200
8. $\frac{1}{10}$ of ☐ = 50p
9. 160 − 80 = ☐

2
1. Explain how to find the number of minutes in any number of hours.
2. A cinema ticket costs £4. Explain how to find the total cost in pounds of any number of tickets.

3 Copy the grid and fill in the missing numbers.

× 6	× 7	× 8	× 9
4 → ☐	3 → ☐	9 → ☐	0 → ☐
8 → ☐	7 → ☐	6 → ☐	10 → ☐
5 → ☐	2 → ☐	4 → ☐	7 → ☐

4
1. A car covers 1 lap of a track in 1 minute 10 seconds. How long will it take to do 4 laps at the same speed?
2. A train leaves Plymouth at 9:50 a.m. and arrives at Birmingham at 12:30 p.m. How long does the journey take?
3. A cafe opens for lunch at 11:30 a.m. and closes 3 hours later. At what time does it close?

5 Choose two digits from the box to make the division. Find the answer.

| 7 | 2 | 5 | 8 |

☐☐0 ÷ 10   Do this 10 times.

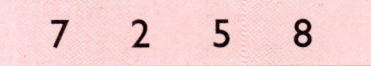

Numeracy Focus 4: Practice Book

Practice 25a

1 Copy these and complete them.

1. Add 10 to 9
2. 1000 minus 710
3. 250 + 750 = ___
4. 2000 ÷ 10 = ___
5. One tenth of £1
6. 215 × 10 = ___
7. 2000 − 1993 = ___
8. Share 33 among 3
9. 6 + 9 + 4 = ___

2 Copy these and complete them.

1. 17 —×3→ ☐ —double→ ☐   17 —×6→ ☐
2. 16 —×4→ ☐ —double→ ☐   16 —×8→ ☐
3. 44 —double→ ☐ —double→ ☐   44 —×4→ ☐

Look for patterns. Explain why they happen.

3 Copy these two calculations.

37 × ☆ = ☐ and (30 × ☆) + (7 × ☆) = ☐

Find the answers when the number hiding behind each star is 4.
Repeat for 5, 6, 7 and 8. Why are the two answers equal each time?

4 Copy the grid. Complete the top and bottom rows.

add 19	56						
number	37	75	157	286	429	563	402
subtract 19	18						

5 Use the five digits in the circle to make this subtraction. Find the answer.

☐☐☐☐ − ☐

Do this ten times.

(5, 6, 7, 8, 9)

Practice 25b

1 Copy these and write the missing numbers.

1. 260 + 260 = ▢
2. ▢ ÷ 100 = 50
3. 17 + 18 + ▢ = 37
4. 21 + ▢ + 22 = 49
5. ▢ + 61 = 136
6. $\frac{1}{5}$ of ▢ = 50p
7. ▢ × 10 = 50
8. 71 + ▢ = 100
9. ▢ − 1000 = 3333

2 Imogen has a rule. To multiply a number by 20, she first doubles the number and then multiplies by 10.

Use Imogen's rule to multiply these numbers by 20.

| 8 | 14 | 32 | 120 | 471 | 208 |

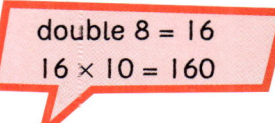

double 8 = 16
16 × 10 = 160

3 Gary uses this diagram to calculate 5 × 17.
How does it work?
Make up six of your own multiplications.
Use Gary's method to find the answer.

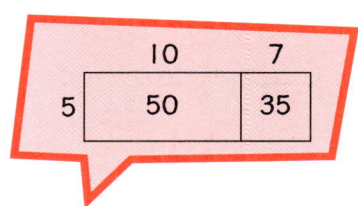

	10	7
5	50	35

4 Copy these and match the calculations which give the same answers.

(2 × 3) —— (3 + 3)
6 × 7
11 × 5
29 × 4
52 × 8

11 + 11 + 11 + 11 + 11
52 + 52 + 52 + 52 + 52 + 52 + 52 + 52
7 + 7 + 7 + 7 + 7 + 7
29 + 29 + 29 + 29

5 Each number in the box is a product of two single-digit numbers greater than 1.
Write each multiplication.

9 × 8 = 72

| 72 | 16 | 24 | 42 | 81 | 54 | 63 | 48 |

Numeracy Focus 4: Practice Book

Practice 26a

1 Copy these and complete them.

1. 100 − 84 = ___
2. 404 × 10 = ___
3. One fifth of £1
4. 65 + 29 = ___
5. Divide 42 by 2
6. 816 − 400 = ___
7. 6000 ÷ 10 = ___
8. 12 + 8 + 6 = ___
9. 31 + 30 = ___

2 Write down the fraction to which each arrow is pointing.

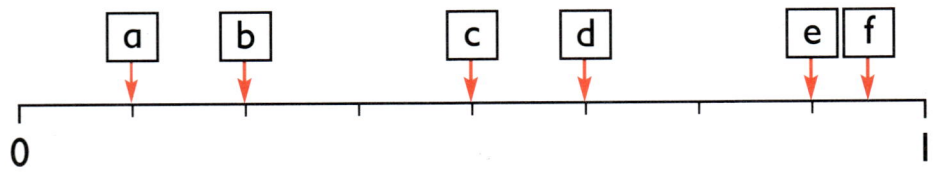

3 Copy these and complete them. Repeated subtraction may help you.

1. 104 ÷ 26 = ___
2. 306 ÷ 51 = ___
3. 245 ÷ 49 = ___
4. 208 ÷ 52 = ___
5. 224 ÷ 56 = ___
6. 504 ÷ 101 = ___

4 Copy these and complete them. Multiplying by 10 may help you.

1. 37 × 11 = ___
2. 43 × 9 = ___
3. 52 × 11 = ___
4. 26 × 9 = ___
5. 64 × 11 = ___
6. 75 × 9 = ___

5 Choose four digits from the box to make this subtraction.

Find the answer.

☐☐☐ − ☐9

| 2 | 3 | 4 | 5 | 6 | 7 |

Do this five times.

Numeracy Focus 4: Practice Book

Practice 26b

1 Copy these and write the missing numbers.

1. ☐ × 1 = 25
2. 394 − ☐ = 194
3. 340 − 170 = ☐
4. 129 + ☐ = 259
5. 400 − ☐ = 393
6. ☐ + 53 = 108
7. ☐ + 59 = 90
8. 4 × 8 = ☐
9. ☐ + 39 = 61

2 Choose a number from the first box and multiply it by a number from the second box.

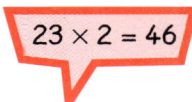
23 × 2 = 46

| 23 | 42 | 34 | 13 | 26 | 44 |

| 2 | 3 | 4 | 5 | 6 |

Do this ten times.

3 Copy these. Use numbers from the circle to complete the multiplications.

6 7 8 9

1. ☐ × 7 = 42
2. ☐ × ☐ = 72
3. 4 × ☐ = 32
4. ☐ × ☐ = 54
5. ☐ × 3 = 27
6. ☐ × ☐ = 56

4 Make up a division by choosing a number from the top box and dividing it by a number from the bottom box. The answer must NOT have a remainder.

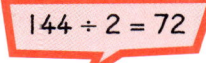
144 ÷ 2 = 72

Write down eight divisions.

| 144 | 208 | 235 | 160 | 180 | 333 | 189 | 207 |

| 2 | 5 | 6 | 3 | 8 | 9 |

5 Copy the diagram. Arrange the numbers 20 30 40 50 60 70 in the circles so that any two numbers connected by a line differ by more than 10.

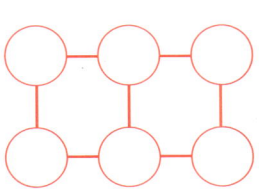

Numeracy Focus 4: Practice Book

Practice 27a

1 Copy these and complete them.

1. 12 − 7 = ___
2. 5002 − 4996 = ___
3. 17 + 12 + 3 = ___
4. 60 ÷ 10 = ___
5. One hundredth of 1000
6. 57 − 19 = ___
7. 230 − 70 = ___
8. 18 + 82 = ___
9. Divide 4 into 48

2

1. The full jar of coffee weighs 400 grams. How much does an empty jar weigh?
2. A box holds 12 jars. What is the weight of 12 full jars of coffee, in kilograms?
3. What fraction of a full jar is the weight of the coffee?

3 Copy and complete these diagrams. Use 5 as the starting number.

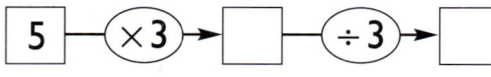

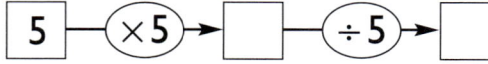

Do the same with these starting numbers. | 6 7 8 9 10 |

4

1. Six children can sit at a table. How many tables are needed for 30 children?
2. A box of 28 crayons is shared equally among 4 children. How many crayons does each child get?
3. Yusuf reads a book every 2 days. How many books can he read in 16 days?

5 Divide each amount in the box by 2, 4, 5 and 10.

| £40   £6   £10.60   £22.40   £37.20   £100   £92.80 |

Practice 27b

1 Copy these and write the missing numbers.

1. $3 \times 0 = \square$
2. $80 \div \square = 8$
3. $200 + 200 = \square$
4. $\square + 140 = 300$
5. $63 - \square = 36$
6. $\square - 4 = 7$
7. $0 \times \square = 0$
8. $\square + 37 = 80$
9. $54 + \square = 100$

2 Copy these, complete the calculations and continue them for five more rows. What patterns do you notice?

| $10 \times 3 =$ | $10 \times 6 =$ | $11 \times 9 =$ | $8 \div 8 =$ |
| $11 \times 3 =$ | $20 \times 6 =$ | $22 \times 9 =$ | $80 \div 8 =$ |

3 Copy the sorting grid. Write the fractions in the box in the correct place on the grid.

$\frac{1}{3}$ $\frac{5}{8}$ $\frac{3}{6}$ $\frac{2}{4}$ $\frac{1}{8}$ $\frac{1}{4}$ $\frac{4}{8}$ $\frac{2}{3}$

less than $\frac{1}{2}$	equal to $\frac{1}{2}$	greater than $\frac{1}{2}$

4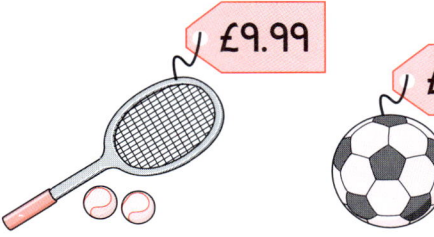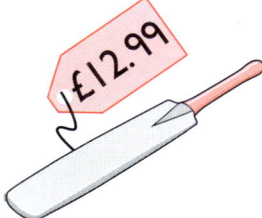

tennis set £9.99   football £6.49   cricket bat £12.99   hockey stick £8.19

Choose two items. Find the total cost. Do this three times.

5 Choose three digits to complete this subtraction. $\boxed{} - \boxed{} = 9$

How many different subtractions can you make if the answer is 9?

Do the same when the answer is 8, 7 and 6.

Practice 28a

1 Copy these and complete them.

1. 45 + 43 = ___
2. Divide 63 by 3
3. 490 × 10 = ___
4. 15 + 16 + 8 = ___
5. 8 times 6
6. Divide 12 by 6
7. 1000 − 450 = ___
8. One half of 1 m
9. 21 ÷ 7 = ___

2 Write these numbers in figures as decimals.

1. seven tenths
2. one and five tenths
3. fifty-two and three tenths
4. one hundred and one tenth
5. two hundred and two and two tenths
6. forty and six tenths

3

1. A school has 315 children. On Monday 29 children go on a school trip. How many are left in the school?
2. A train can hold 237 passengers. There are already 78 passengers on the train. How many more can the train hold?
3. There are 524 books in a library. The children borrow 56 books. How many books are left?

4 Copy these patterns. Write about each of them.

10 + 1 = 11	100 − 1 = 99	7 × 1 = 7	3 − 3 = 0
10 + 2 = 12	200 − 2 = 198	29 × 1 = 29	42 − 42 = 0
10 + 3 = 13	300 − 3 = 297	58 × 1 = 58	18 − 18 = 0
10 + 4 = 14	400 − 4 = 396	146 × 1 = 146	100 − 100 = 0

5 Write ten fractions which have 1 as a numerator.

Put the fractions in order, largest first.

Practice 28b

1 Copy these and write the missing numbers.

1. 87 + 13 − ☐ = 87
2. 7 × 6 = ☐
3. 18 ÷ 6 = ☐
4. 45 ÷ 5 = ☐
5. 16 ÷ ☐ = 8
6. 1200 − 600 = ☐
7. 56 ÷ 7 = ☐
8. ☐ ÷ 3 = 9
9. 71 + ☐ = 90

2 Copy these boxes. Match each decimal with the fraction that has the same value.

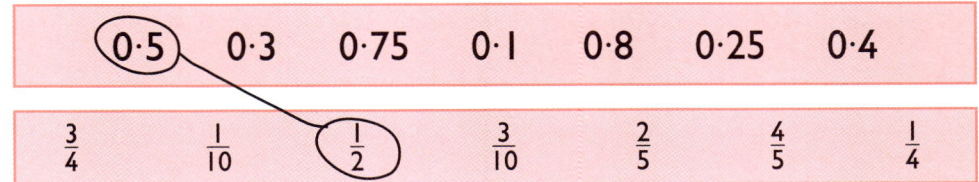

3 Write about where you can see horizontal and vertical lines in your classroom.

4
1. Which day comes three days after Friday?
2. What is the date four weeks before 5th July?
3. What time is 72 minutes before five to one in the afternoon?
4. How many days is it from 12th September to 12th October?
5. How many years are there in a millennium?

5 Copy this sorting diagram.

Write two numbers in each region of the diagram.

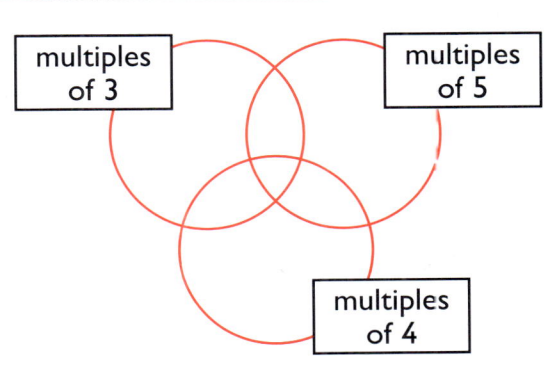

Numeracy Focus 4: Practice Book

Practice 29a

1 Copy these and complete them.
1. 20 + 7 + 30 = ___
2. 9 × 3 = ___
3. 550 + 450 = ___
4. 28 divided by 2
5. 24 ÷ 6 = ___
6. 18 divided by 9
7. One half of 78
8. 8100 ÷ 10 = ___
9. 56 add 81

2
1. Draw a grid which has three horizontal and four vertical lines.
2. Draw a grid which has three rows and four columns.
3. Draw a polygon that has two diagonals.
4. Draw a polygon that has five diagonals.

3
1. Which three coins total 50p?
2. Which four coins total £3.05?
3. Which five coins total £4.17?
4. Which six coins total £2.73?

4 Choose digits from the box to make two decimal numbers which are:
1. between 5 and 6
2. more than 4·1 and less than 4·5
3. between 3 and 3·3

| 1 | 2 | 3 | 4 |
| 5 | 6 | 7 | 8 |

5 Draw three copies of this 4 × 4 grid.

Shade squares to make a shape which has:
1. one line of symmetry
2. two lines of symmetry
3. a diagonal line of symmetry

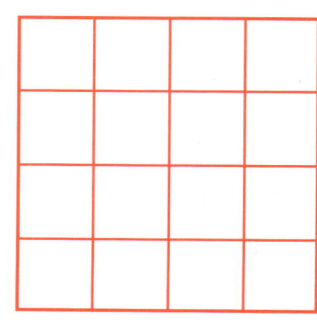
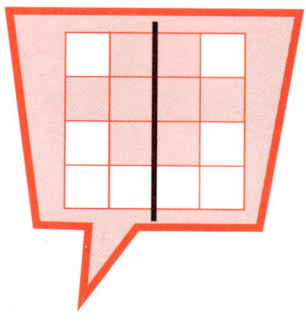

Practice 29b

1 Copy these and write the missing numbers.

1. 1600 − ☐ = 900
2. 14 ÷ 7 = ☐
3. 28 ÷ ☐ = 7
4. 62 − 15 + ☐ = 62
5. 8 × 9 = ☐
6. ☐ ÷ 5 = 7
7. 4000 + 4000 = ☐
8. 24 ÷ 8 = ☐
9. 3000 − ☐ = 4

2 Write the directions in which these aeroplanes are pointing.

1 → south

1 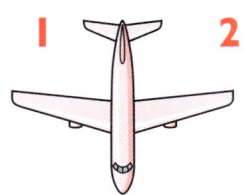 2  3  4  5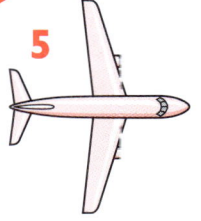

N ↑

3 Write the amounts from each circle in order, smallest to largest.

- 3·2, 4·1, 1·4, 0·9, 2·3
- 88p, £1.08, 8p, £0.70, 80p
- 5·4 kg, 0·45 kg, 0·5 kg, 1·03 kg, 3·1 kg
- 7·8 m, 0·08 m, 0·87 m, 0·78 m, 8·7 m

4 Copy the grid.

Write the sum of pairs of numbers that are next to each other. Do this for all 12 pairs.

4165 + 7 = 4172

4165	7	3038
8	9297	6
1283	9	6999

5 Copy the diagram.

Write the numbers 1 to 12 in the squares so that the two columns of four numbers each total 26 and the two rows of four numbers each total 30.

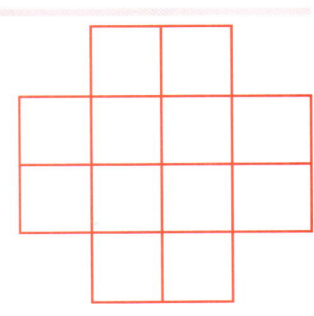

Numeracy Focus 4: Practice Book

Practice 30a

1 Copy these and complete them.

1. 13 + 11 + 9 = ____
2. 84 divided by 4
3. 8 times 4
4. 49 ÷ 7 = ____
5. One quarter of 1 m
6. Share 16 among 8
7. 29 × 100 = ____
8. 6 multiplied by 6
9. 1000 − 850 = ____

2

1. A racing car takes 1 minute 15 seconds to do a lap of the track. How long will it take to do 4 laps?
2. A jumbo jet travels 500 miles in one hour. How many hours will it take to travel 3000 miles?
3. Sound travels at 1200 km per hour. How many minutes will it take for sound to travel 200 kilometres?

3 The odd number in the oval is between the odd numbers in the squares. Find the missing odd numbers.

1. ☐ − 39 − ☐
2. ☐ − 147 − ☐
3. ☐ − 373 − ☐
4. ☐ − 1001 − ☐
5. ☐ − 8301 − ☐
6. ☐ − 9999 − ☐

4 Copy the diagram.

What are the coordinates of the vertices of the square?

What are the coordinates of the intersection of the diagonals of the square?

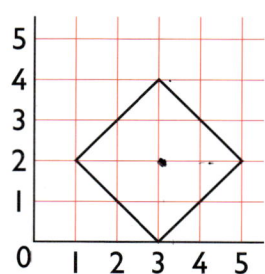

5 Use the digits 3 4 5 to make six decimal numbers which have ones and tenths.

Put your six numbers in order.

Practice 30b

1 Copy these and write the missing numbers.

1. ☐ × 2 = 80
2. 36 ÷ 6 = ☐
3. 42 ÷ 7 = ☐
4. 5 × 9 = ☐
5. 30 ÷ ☐ = 3
6. 8 × 7 = ☐
7. 42 + ☐ = 70
8. 4400 − 2200 = ☐
9. 800 + 60 − ☐ = 800

2 Copy the grid and the shaded figure.

Write the coordinates of each of the lettered points.

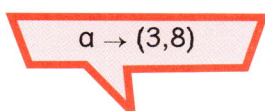

a → (3,8)

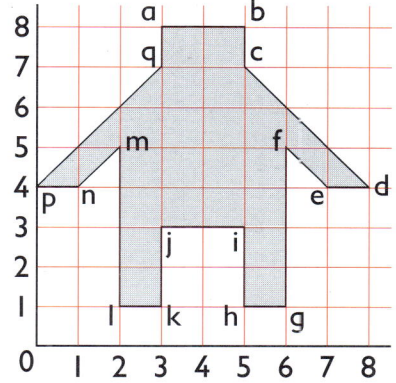

3 Choose four digits from 8 4 2 6 0 to make a 4-digit number.

Make six more 4-digit numbers.

Put your seven numbers in order, largest first. Leave gaps between them.

In each gap, write a number which is halfway between the two numbers.

4
1. How many biscuits are there in 4 packets?
2. If 17 biscuits are eaten from a full packet, how many are left?
3. Rachel puts one quarter of a full packet on a plate. How many biscuits are there on the plate?

24 Chocolate Biscuits

5 Use the digits 3 9 5 7 to make 12 different 2-digit numbers.

Write the twelve numbers in pairs and find the six differences.
Why are the differences always even?

Numeracy Focus 4: Practice Book

Practice 31a

1 Copy these and complete them.

1. 9 times 6 = ___
2. 350 + 650 = ___
3. Add 11 to 6
4. Share 120 among 10
5. 20 + 40 + 30 = ___
6. 2911 − 7 = ___
7. 54 ÷ 6 = ___
8. 20 × 10 = ___
9. Increase 38 by 22

2 Copy the numbers in the box. Write them in order.

$$-5 \quad -8 \quad -1 \quad 0 \quad -3 \quad -6$$

Show the position of the numbers on a number line that goes from −10 to 0.

3 Find the sum and the difference between each pair of numbers.

Check your answers using the odd and even number rules.

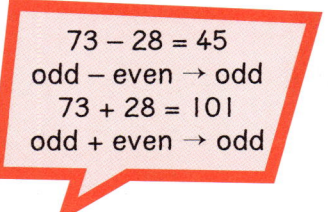

73 − 28 = 45
odd − even → odd
73 + 28 = 101
odd + even → odd

1. 73, 28
2. 41, 65
3. 59, 92
4. 14, 66
5. 86, 39
6. 77, 48

4 Look at the diagram.

1. Find three numbers that total 36. How many ways can you do this?
2. Find four numbers that total 37. How many ways can you do this?
3. Find five numbers that total 38. How many ways can you do this?

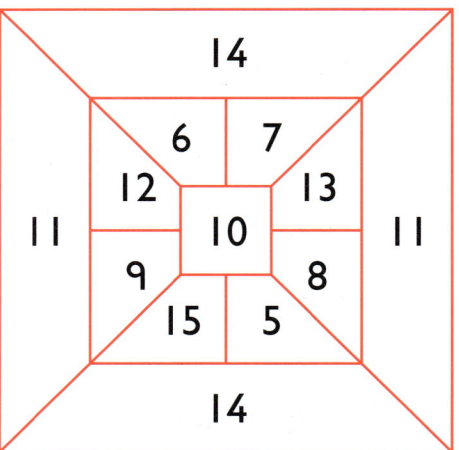

5 Write four fractions that have the same value as 0·5.

Do the same for 0·1, 0·25 and 0·75.

Numeracy Focus 4: Practice Book

Practice 31b

1 Copy these and write the missing numbers.

1. Half of ▢ = 560
2. 1 ÷ ▢ = 1
3. 6 × 9 = ▢
4. 42 ÷ 6 = ▢
5. 900 ÷ ▢ = 90
6. 54 ÷ 9 = ▢
7. ▢ ÷ 1 = 50
8. ▢ + 19 = 63
9. ½ of ▢ = 20p

2 Choose a number from each circle.
Find the difference.
Check your answer by adding.
Do this ten times.

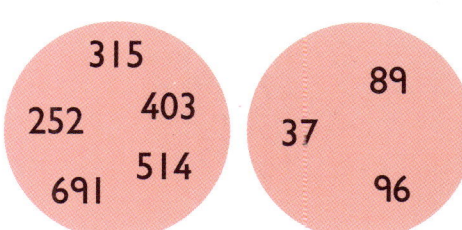

3 Here are five 4-digit numbers. Use each of the digits in the box to complete the five numbers so that they are in order, largest first.

2	2	2	3	3
3	3	4	4	4

▢ ▢ 4 7 ▢ ▢ 4 7 ▢ ▢ 4 7 ▢ ▢ 4 7 ▢ ▢ 4 7

4 Copy the grid.

Round each number to the nearest 10 and to the nearest 100.

nearest 10	370							
number	369	298	951	107	649	703	825	276
nearest 100	400							

5 Using cm-squared paper, draw ten different shapes which each enclose 36 squares.

What is the perimeter of each shape?

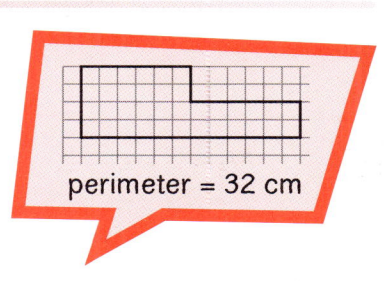

perimeter = 32 cm

Practice 32a

1 Copy these and complete them.

1. 71 + 29 = ___
2. 63 ÷ 9 = ___
3. 3000 subtract 8
4. 82 − 29 = ___
5. 9 times 7
6. 65 divided by 5
7. 32 ÷ 8 = ___
8. 70 + 80 − 80 = ___
9. 420 ÷ 10 = ___

2 Find the sum of each pair of numbers.

1. 47, 29
2. 56, 35
3. 18, 84
4. 28, 63
5. 34, 39
6. 73, 29

3

1. How much more than the soccer goal does the skateboard cost?
2. Naomi has £100. Which two could she buy? What change would she get?
3. What is the total cost of the three items?

4 Copy these and write the signs (+, −, × or ÷) that are hiding behind the stars.

1. 48 ☆ 6 = 8
2. 36 ☆ 28 = 64
3. 3 ☆ 17 = 51
4. 300 ☆ 50 = 6
5. 450 ☆ 125 = 325
6. 23 ☆ 3 = 69

5 Using squared paper, draw four different rectangles that cover 48 squares.

Practice 32b

1 Copy these and write the missing numbers.

1. $7 \times 7 = \square$
2. $63 \div 7 = \square$
3. $\frac{1}{4}$ of $\square = 25p$
4. $\square + 19 + 11 = 46$
5. $36 \div 9 = \square$
6. $40 + 50 + \square = 100$
7. $180 \div \square = 90$
8. $610 \times \square = 6100$
9. Half of $\square = 8000$

2 Use the numbers ⟨3 9 5 8⟩ and the operations + and × to make ten different calculations.

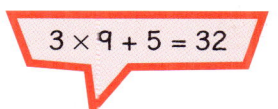
$3 \times 9 + 5 = 32$

3 Choose one number from each circle.

Find the sum and the difference of the two numbers.

Check your answers by using the inverse operation.

Do this six times.

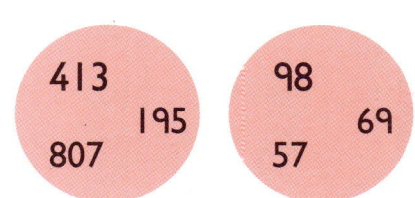

4 Measure the lengths of the sides of these shapes, to the nearest millimetre.

What is the perimeter of each shape?

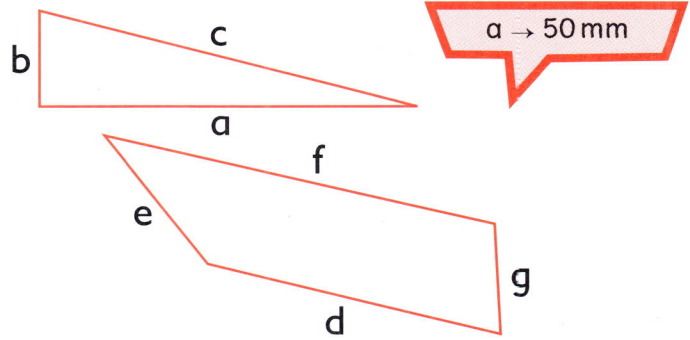

a → 50 mm

5 Draw a rectangle.

Investigate ways of drawing two straight lines to partition the rectangle in different ways.

List the names of the shapes each time.

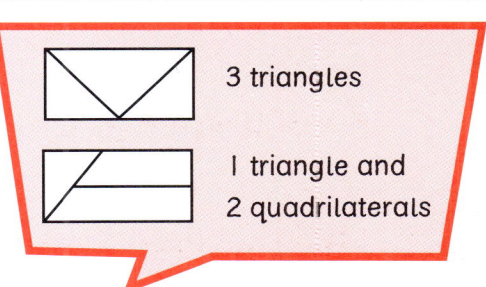

3 triangles

1 triangle and 2 quadrilaterals

65

Numeracy Focus 4: Practice Book

Practice 33a

1 Copy these and complete them.

1. 93 − 48 + 48 = ____
2. 300 × 10 = ____
3. 48 ÷ 6 = ____
4. 7 × 4 = ____
5. One tenth of 1 m
6. Divide 80 by 5
7. 1000 − 250 = ____
8. 35 ÷ 7 = ____
9. One half of 130

2 There are 100 straws in a box.

1. How many straws are there in 20 boxes?
2. A quarter of the straws in the box are blue. How many straws are blue?
3. One box is opened at a party, 73 straws are used. How many are left in the box?

3 Choose one number from each circle and make a multiplication.

Do this ten times.

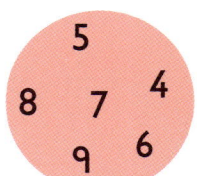

5 × 8 = 40

4 Copy these and fill in the missing numbers.

1. 1 whole turn = ☐ right angles
2. ☐ degrees = 1 right angle
3. 90 degrees = ☐ of a turn
4. 3 right angles = ☐ of a turn
5. ½ of a turn = ☐ degrees

5 Use the digits in the box to complete the addition and the subtraction.

0 1 2 3 4 5 6 7 8 9

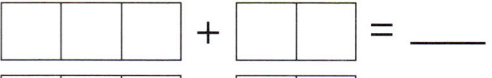 + = ____

 −  = ____   Do this six times.

305 + 76 = 381
182 − 49 = 133

Practice 33b

1 Copy these and write the missing numbers.

1. ☐ ÷ 10 = 40
2. $\frac{1}{10}$ of ☐ = 25 cm
3. 56 ÷ 8 = ☐
4. One hundredth of ☐ = 80
5. 63 − ☐ = 34
6. ☐ ÷ 3 = 80
7. 9 × 4 = ☐
8. 81 ÷ 9 = ☐
9. Half of ☐ = 2600

2 Do these subtractions.

1. 36 − 17
2. 52 − 29
3. 85 − 48
4. 73 − 36
5. 44 − 18
6. 67 − 49

3 Write the amount of turn in right angles, and the direction of turn.

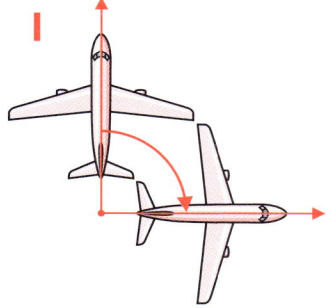
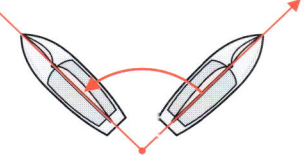
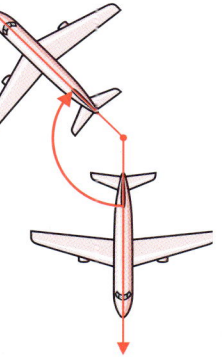

4 There are 200 dog biscuits in a 1 kilogram packet.

1. How many biscuits are there in a 10 kg box?
2. How many grams does 1 biscuit weigh?
3. A dog has 10 biscuits each day. How many days will a packet last?

5 Use the digits 2 3 4 5 6 to complete the addition.

Find the addition which gives the largest possible answer.

☐☐☐ + ☐☐

Practice 34a

1 Copy these and complete them.

1. 30 ÷ 6 = ____
2. 6 multiplied by 3
3. 7148 add 6
4. One tenth of 6000
5. 50 + 60 − 60 = ____
6. Divide 660 by 2
7. 7 times 6
8. 48 ÷ 8 = ____
9. 800 + 400 = ____

2 Find the totals. Check by rounding each amount to the nearest 10p.

1. £3.14 + £2.93
2. £8.57 + £5.24
3. £7.42 + £7.18
4. £6.99 + £10.99

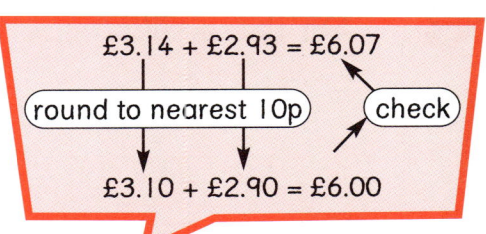

£3.14 + £2.93 = £6.07
round to nearest 10p — check
£3.10 + £2.90 = £6.00

3 Make up a number story for each calculation.

1. 78 − 29 = 49
2. 130 ÷ 10 = 13
3. Double 40 = 80
4. 256 + 37 = 293

4 Copy these angles and fill in the missing numbers.

1. ¼ of a turn
2. ½ of a turn
3. ¾ of a turn

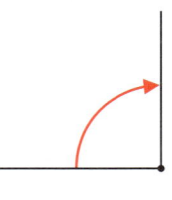 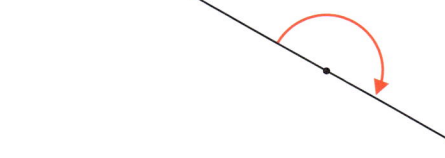 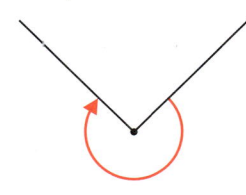

☐ degrees   ☐ degrees   ☐ degrees

☐ right angles   ☐ right angles   ☐ right angles

5 Copy this triangle.

Draw two straight lines in the triangle to make a quadrilateral and two triangles.

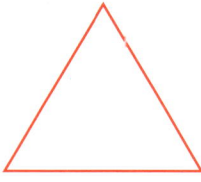

Numeracy Focus 4: Practice Book

Practice 34b

1 Copy these and write the missing numbers.

1. $40 \div 8 = \square$
2. $\square - 39 = 46$
3. $8 \times 8 = \square$
4. $9 \times 8 = \square$
5. $240 \div \square = 60$
6. $28 \div 7 = \square$
7. $\square + 17 + 3 = 26$
8. $\square \times 10 = 3140$
9. $\frac{1}{5}$ of $\square = 25\,g$

2 Write the number of degrees and whether the turn is clockwise or anticlockwise.

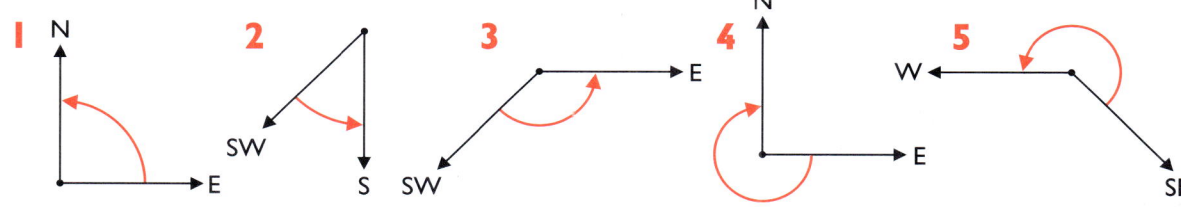

3 Use the calendar for these questions.

1. How many Tuesdays were there in March?
2. On what day of the week was the last day in March?
3. On what day of the week was the last day in February?

	MARCH				
S		6	13	20	27
M		7	14	21	28
T	1	8	15	22	29
W	2	9	16	23	30
T	3	10	17	24	31
F	4	11	18	25	
S	5	12	19	26	

4 On cm-squared paper, draw as many different rectangles as you can with a perimeter of 32 centimetres.

Write the area of each rectangle, in cm².

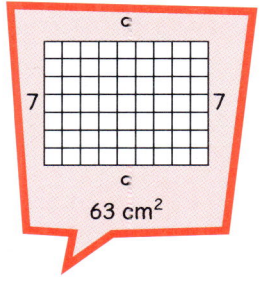

63 cm²

5 Use five of these digits 2 3 5 6 7 8 for this addition so that it has the largest possible answer.

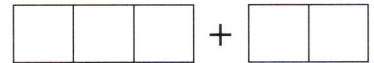

Practice 35a

19/07/08

1 Copy these and complete them.

1. 390 divided by 3
2. 6 × 8 = ___
3. 64 ÷ 8 = ___
4. 37 + 71 = ___
5. One fifth of 1 m
6. 47 + 20 = ___
7. 68 − 30 = ___
8. 80 add 37
9. Add 240 to 29

2 Write three examples for each general statement.

1. The sum of two odd numbers is always an even number.
2. A multiple of 4 is always an even number.
3. A multiple of 10 ends in 0.

3 Start at any corner and follow the lines. End at a different corner. Add the numbers in each square you visit. You cannot visit a square twice.
Find the highest possible score.

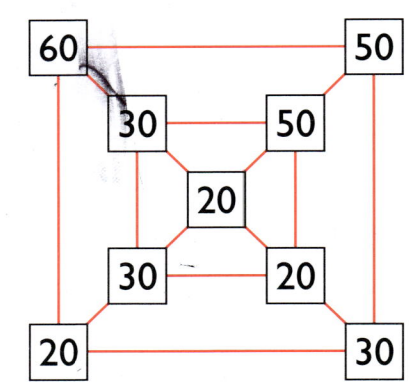

4 Use the three numbers in each box to write two multiplications and two divisions.

15 × 7 = 105   7 × 15 = 105
105 ÷ 7 = 15   105 ÷ 15 = 7

| 15   7 | 12   9 | 112   8 | 96 | 70 1400 |
| 105 | 108 | 14 | 6   16 | 20 |

5 Choose five digits from the circle for the addition.

Find the answer.

Do this four times.

Circle digits: 3, 6, 7, 5, 9, 8, 4

Numeracy Focus 4: Practice Book

Practice 36a

1 Copy these and complete them.

1. 9010 ÷ 10 = ____
2. 7 times 9
3. 45 ÷ 9 = ____
4. 71 − 43 = ____
5. 629 + 50 = ____
6. 7000 + 605 = ____
7. Divide 600 by 4
8. 351 − 40 = ____
9. 400 + 158 = ____

2 Divide each number in the box by 6, 7, 8 and 9. Write the answer to the division with a remainder.

| 13 | 17 | 22 | 29 | 31 | 58 | 75 |

13 ÷ 6 = 2 rem 1
13 ÷ 7 = 1 rem 6
13 ÷ 8 = 1 rem 5
13 ÷ 9 = 1 rem 4

3 Copy the grid. Double and halve each number.

double	100						
number	50	400	140	320	1000	680	500
halve	25						

4
1. A box holds 12 bottles. How many are needed for 90 bottles?
2. A cake is cut into 6 pieces. How many cakes are needed for 40 children each to have a piece?
3. How many 8 cm lengths can be cut from a 1 m stick?

5 Draw three circles. Put three numbers from the box in each circle so that each circle has a total of 1500.

| 100 | 200 | 300 | 400 | 500 | 600 | 700 | 800 | 900 |

Find different ways of doing this.

Numeracy Focus 4: Practice Book

Practice 35b

1 Copy these and write the missing numbers.

1. 40 + ☐ = 63
2. 6 × 7 = ☐
3. ☐ ÷ 5 = 110
4. ☐ − 20 = 77
5. ☐ ÷ 10 = 3000
6. ☐ + 21 = 341
7. ☐ + 36 = 86
8. 27 ÷ 9 = ☐
9. 60 + ☐ + 80 = 200

2 Copy these diagrams and complete them.

The number in a circle is the sum of the two numbers in the boxes either side of the circle.

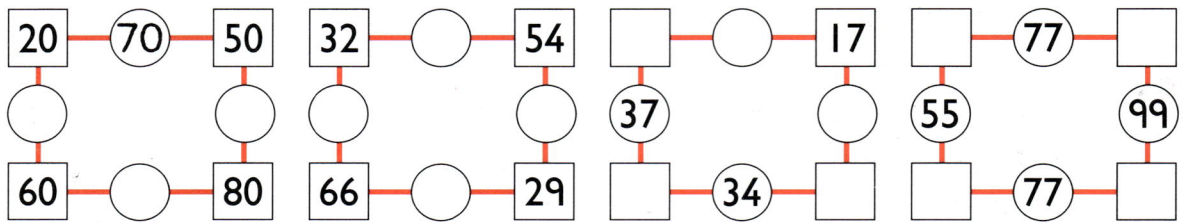

3 Copy and complete this diagram.

| 27 | 8 | 49 | 66 | 183 | 50 |

Choose a start number from the box.

☐ —×100→ ☐ —÷10→ ☐ —×10→ ☐ —÷100→ ☐

Do this six times. What do you notice? Explain why it happens.

4 You will need a 45° set square, a 60° set square and a ruler.

Use your set squares and ruler to draw these shapes.

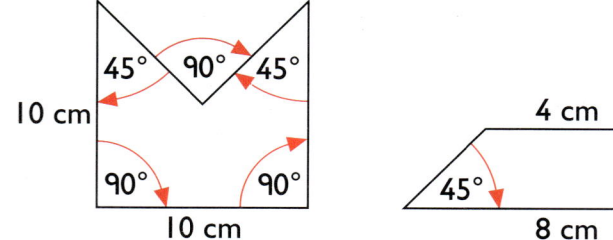 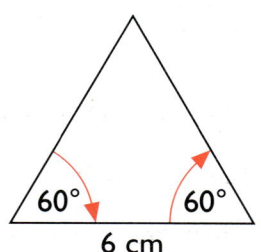

Now draw a pentagon, a hexagon and an octagon.

Practice 36b

1 Copy these and write the missing numbers.

1. 6700 + ☐ = 7000
2. ☐ + 70 + 50 = 150
3. ☐ ÷ 10 = 30
4. ☐ + 60 = 488
5. 600 + ☐ = 771
6. 390 ÷ ☐ = 39
7. 282 − ☐ = 222
8. ☐ + 315 = 6315
9. 9 × 9 = ☐

2 Melina has a rule. To find a quarter of any number she halves the number and halves the answer.

Use Melina's rule to find a quarter of each of the numbers in the box.

| 84 | 108 | 188 | 264 | 392 | 1004 |

$\frac{1}{2}$ of 84 = 42

$\frac{1}{2}$ of 42 = 21

$\frac{1}{4}$ of 84 = 21

3 Make up four divisions which have a remainder of 1. Do the same for remainders 2, 3 and 4.

7 ÷ 3 = 2 rem 1

4 Copy the grid. Halve each number three times.

number	8	24	56	120	224	320	488
halve	4						
halve again	2						
halve again	1						

5 Multiply the numbers in the box by 2.

| 1 2 3 4 5 6 7 8 9 |

Are the answers even or odd?

What if you multiply the numbers by 3, 4, 5, 6, 7, 8, 9, 10?

Write about what you notice. Explain why.

Numeracy Focus 4: Practice Book